Bittersweet Berries

GROWING UP JEWISH IN MINNESOTA

Bittersweet Berries

GROWING UP JEWISH
IN
MINNESOTA

by Ruth F. Brin

HOLY COW! PRESS · DULUTH, MINNESOTA · 1999

The publisher gratefully acknowledges the editorial assistance of Jan Zita
Grover and David Brin in preparing the text of this book.

An early version of Chapter Six, "The Milkman, the Iceman, and
Ice Chips in the Sawdust at the Bottom of the Wagon," appeared
in *Ramsey County History.*

First Printing, 1999
10 9 8 7 6 5 4 3 2 1

Library of Congress Cataloging-in-Publication Data
Brin, Ruth Firestone
    Bittersweet berries : growing up Jewish in Minnesota / by Ruth F. Brin.
    p.   cm.
    ISBN 0-930100-83-2
    1. Brin, Ruth Firestone—Childhood and youth. 2. Jews—Minnesota-
-St. Paul—Biography. 3. Saint Paul (Minn.)—Biography.
    I. Title
F614.S4B75   1999
977.6' 581004924' 0092—dc21
[B]   98-47111
                                                 CIP

Publisher's Address:
HOLY COW! PRESS
Post Office Box 3170
Mount Royal Station
Duluth, Minnesota 55803

Holy Cow! Press books are distributed to the trade by Consortium Book Sales
& Distribution, 1045 Westgate Drive, Saint Paul, Minnesota 55114.

This publication was supported in part by a grant from the Arrowhead
Regional Arts Council through an appropriation from the Minnesota
State Legislature, Elmer L. Andersen, and by generous individuals.

To all who went before,

especially my beloved husband, Howard, whose staunch and loving support helped me to grow and write and helped our four children to become wise, giving adults,

and to all who come after,
especially those who want to know this story.

Contents

Introduction

I grew up in St. Paul in the 1920s and '30s in a middle-class Jewish family, mostly functioning well in spite of difficulties. Does that make my story typical of middle-class people in those days? Of girls of the time? Of Jews? I don't think so. The Jewish life in St. Paul's West Side, capitol neighborhood and Selby-Dale may have been quite different from my adventures in Midway—and more Jews at that time lived in those neighborhoods. Not many girls grew up in the 1920s with a college-educated mother who had worked for suffrage and birth control and who believed in women's rights. That alone made my girlhood experiences different. And as for the middle class, that category is so broad that it defies any attempt to tell a typical story. This is a memoir of how I grew up, and I hope it will be read as the story of an individual.

Writing a memoir immediately raises a much more difficult question than: am I typical? That more difficult question is, "What is the truth?" I can't check this out with my parents or my brother George, because they died many years ago. My brother Linn, five years older than I, still lives in St. Paul and remembers things I can't recall, but this account is based on my own memories. Memory is selective, tends to make us more heroic than we are, to paint childhood as happier than it was. I will try to include the tough with the tender, the sorrows as well as the joys. Growing up is never easy, and this is my story, truth filtered through memory.

—Ruth F. Brin
Minneapolis, Minnesota
December, 1997

I

PROLOGUE

Irma's Dream

When I was a very little girl, my mother, Irma, convinced me that I was having a happy childhood, especially compared to hers. And she was right. Mostly, I was a contented child in a "happy family," but no family is happy all the time, and every child has black periods. My mother had a hard time growing up, and that had a major effect on me.

Irma's mother had become sick after the birth of her baby brother Milford, who was eight years younger than Irma. Their mother died when Milford was a year old and Irma nine. Although her father could afford to hire maids or housekeepers, Irma's life had been chaotic. She often was left alone to take care of the baby. Irma's mother had been the youngest of a large family who had come from Germany. Every time the little girl developed a friendship with one of the young Irish immigrant girls who were available as domestic help in the 1890s in Chicago, her aunts would find dust on the bookcase. The girl would be fired and Irma would lose a friend.

Her father tried to help but he worked long hours. The aunts would scold if she hadn't taken her brother for a walk in his buggy, a task she hated. Her aunts were thrifty and bought her shoes and dresses too big so she would grow into them. She was terribly embarrassed when she graduated from eighth grade because the sleeves of her required white dress were so long that they covered her hands. She had to wear the same dress the following fall at a family wedding, and by then she felt even worse because it was too short and too tight in "the chest."

All her life, it seemed, Irma missed her own mother and wished for a sister or a dear woman friend whom she never seemed to find. When she started high school, her father decided he had to hire a woman to take care of Milford, who was an unhappy and difficult little boy; this woman could also supervise the maid. Meddy Helfaer was a German-Jewish woman from Milwaukee who had studied the Froebel method of kindergarten teaching. My mother liked her and she was wonderful with Milford; he loved her, called her "Mutti" (mother) and his behavior improved immensely. Two years later my grandfather, whose own parents were from French Alsace, married Meddy. By then, Irma was a senior in high school and ready to go to Vassar College in the fall. The new mother had arrived too late for her.

Although this story seems to have a happy ending, there were problems. My grandfather had been working for his in-laws in their spice and hops business. When he married Meddy several years after the death of his wife, his in-laws were so angry they immediately threw him out of the business. Irma lost contact, not only with her interfering aunts, but also with cousins whom she liked. She did keep in touch with her favorite, Jessie, who later left Chicago to marry a German Jew and live with him in Frankfurt Am Main. Irma's father started his own business in competition with his in-laws, selling hops to breweries and spices to sausage-makers.

There was a sad, dark place in my mother, a lonely hollow that had never been filled since her own mother died. Her loving husband and two little boys hadn't entirely filled that void. When she was pregnant with me she was dreaming of a daughter who would be beautiful, strong, long-legged, with auburn hair and dark eyes. This daughter would grow up able to vote and to have a more exciting career than Irma, whose ambitions had been curtailed by woman's place in the nineteenth century. This daughter would be the companion she had sought for so long.

My mother had this dream of a tall daughter in spite of the fact that she and Dad were both only a little over five feet tall. Mother had wavy chestnut brown hair and soft brown eyes behind the pince-nez she wore in those days. Her difficult childhood had included surgery to correct crossed eyes, and this left her "wall-eyed" (looking out instead of in). Similarly unsuccessful orthodonture that had left her with a crooked bite. She was convinced she was homely; since she said so, I thought so, too, and was sure that I, too, was ugly.

My father, already bald when he began to court my mother, had snapping dark eyes and flared nostrils, a clue to his excitable nature. He had broad shoulders and a deep voice. In my childhood he always wore wool suits and white shirts with stiff collars. He liked to wear a flower in his buttonhole in the summer. He simply hoped for a little girl because he had two boys.

When my father drove her to Miller Hospital on May 5,

1921, Mother's labor with me was short. In the delivery room, she was greeted by an old friend, Harrie Solomon, the chief obstetrical nurse, who proceeded to deliver me in the absence of the doctor. In Harrie's honor, I was named Ruth Harrie Firestone, to my consternation years later, when my brothers liked to spell my middle name "hairy."

When my mother first saw me, she must have been disappointed. I wasn't red and crying lustily like her older two newborns. Harrie had to slap me to get me to squawk; I not only had a scrawny body and scraggly black hair hanging over my face, but I was a sickly yellow color. Mother thought there was something terribly wrong with me, but Harrie reassured her that jaundice of the newborn was common and not serious.

Mother's dream daughter was eclipsed that day at Miller Hospital. Still her dream haunted not only my mother in years to come, but me, too. Sometimes I would struggle to be her missing sister or friend, or even after I grew up, her missing mother, to fill that dark loneliness. At other times, I would reject her dream with all my might.

2

Up Against Medical Science

Of course my mother, a well-educated woman and a graduate of Vassar College, believed that medicine was a science and that she must follow the rules of her pediatrician, T. L. Birnberg, especially as he had studied not only in Minnesota but in Vienna as well. Everyone knew German medical science was the best, and these were the rules: Even if the baby cries, you only feed her every four hours. No more. She is supposed to take four ounces and you weigh her before and after breast feeding to check on this. As she grows older, you add cereal and other solids and drop the 2 a.m. feeding. The child should double her birth weight in six months and triple it by one year. After she is on solid food, which in the 1920s meant that Mother personally strained all the vegetables, fruits, and meats—certain foods were required for proper nutrition. If she doesn't eat them, you keep her in the high chair until she does, even for hours.

What if the baby is small and doesn't want four ounces? And what if she cries after three hours? You keep trying to feed her on the fourth hour, and by then she's so exhausted she falls asleep after two ounces. Picking up a crying child was also frowned on. If the child is not wet and no diaper pin is sticking in her, and the four hours haven't passed, then picking her up is forbidden. Verboten.

Irma followed the rules and I, Ruth Harrie, didn't. I cried; I spit out solid food. I didn't gain weight as quickly as I was supposed to. I cried so much at night that Mother relented and nursed me. The doctor was angry and labeled me a feeding problem. Irma thought I might be backward. I didn't learn to crawl. When I was a year old I would sit on the floor and push myself along, one hand in front of me, one in back. I didn't weigh much—my brother George, a sturdy four year old, could easily pick me up. Linn, at six and a half, ignored us both. But skinny and uncoordinated as I was, I began to talk as early as my brothers had.

In the second year of my life, Irma's problems weren't over. Linn developed such bad eczema that he attended first grade somewhat irregularly. Mother taught him at home—she had taught plenty of first-grade classes in the Chicago public schools. He was soon reading. Then her stepmother, Meddy, who lived in Chicago, became ill. Linn had nicknamed this slight, white-haired grandmother "Donny" and so she remained.

Donny was not ill enough for a hospital and not well enough to live alone. She came to the house at 1866 Portland Avenue and was installed in the sunroom, our playroom. She and my father got along well; I didn't know until I was grown that she had objected to the marriage because my Dad's parents were Hungarian, not German, but she had quickly reconciled herself to it. I was about 18 months old when Donny arrived.

Irma thought it best to hire a "baby nurse" for me and the boys while she would take care of Donny herself. The nurse was called Johnnie because her last name was Johnson. Johnnie tried to follow the rules for creating feeding problems out of ordinary young children and almost succeeded as well as Irma.

I do remember when I first walked, not because I have such a remarkable memory, but because I was so old. Mother thought I hadn't started to walk because I was little and weak. Or maybe because Johnnie carried me around so much. Or maybe because sometimes the boys knocked me down when I tried to stand up. Little boys can be rough accidentally or on purpose. On the other hand, I was talking quite a bit and I informed Mother that I wanted a baby buggy for my doll for my second birthday present. I wanted a little one that I could play with while I was sitting on the floor.

After a while my stern mother told me that I couldn't have a baby buggy unless I would try to walk. I had no intentions of walking because it was so frightening. But this is what I remember: On the morning of my second birthday, I was wearing a white romper and white high-button shoes, the kind you closed with a button hook. I crawled backwards down the stairs from my bedroom to the living room and sat on the bottom step. My mother was sitting in a green chair looking at me. If I pushed off from the bottom step I was going to have to step on some scary red things on the Oriental rug—when I pushed myself along the floor I always went around them. But I needed the step to get up. And I did it! I took two-and-a-half steps, felt tall and dizzy, and fell on the rug.

Mother told me she picked me up right away and hugged and kissed me. She also admitted she had hidden the buggy in the basement and was really worried that I wouldn't try to walk. Then what would she do? Finally, she had bought a rather large doll buggy so I must stand up to push it, and that was really how I learned to walk.

My early childhood was not free of the pediatrician either. By the time I was four I absolutely hated Dr. Birnberg. I associated waiting in his office with a still life that hung on his wall of a hunter's quarry—a hanging stag and droopy geese. I expected he might want to do to me what the hunter had done to the animals.

When we got into his office he would talk gruffly to my mother as though I wasn't there, or was some peculiar specimen of primitive life; he never approved of anything about me. Dire warnings, pokes, and commands to open my mouth wide. I was too short, I didn't weigh enough, I wasn't growing enough. My mother would leave distressed and unhappy and more determined than ever to make me eat. I can remember being scolded for not eating enough, being told I wouldn't grow, and having to swallow stinking cod liver oil by the tablespoonful. I wasn't allowed to play or later to go to school, until I had a bowel movement after breakfast. Mother even wrote letters to her cousin in Germany comparing the merits of prunes and St. John's bread.

My house was a three-story stucco house with a front porch where we would sit on summer evenings. Like all small children I followed my mother around. I could sit on the blue-and-white linoleum under the kitchen sink, which was white enamel on tall iron legs, and listen to the exposed pipes gurgle when Mother or the maid washed dishes. My high chair would be pulled up to the white enamel kitchen table near the chip on the edge for breakfast and lunch. At dinner time the high chair would appear in the dining room where I could see myself in the mirror on the dark oak sideboard.

Dinner was best because there would be at least one thing I liked to eat and Mother and Dad and the boys would get into big discussions and maybe they would forget to tell me I wasn't eating enough. I looked forward to dessert. Donny watched me one day and advised mother to get a green rug so the spinach I was spilling wouldn't show.

There were some mysterious places in my house. When I sat on the little white hexagonal tiles in the upstairs bathroom, I could look at a door about a foot high. When Mother opened it she always cautioned me to stay away and not fall down the opening. I could see it was black down there. Sometimes she pushed dirty clothes or sheets into that door. There was a pile of dirty laundry in the basement, but it took me a long time to connect the two.

There was a little back hall off the kitchen called a vestibule. When children played outside, they had to come in the back door to this hall and hang their coats on the hooks. On the other side was the wooden ice chest. If I looked in the top, which was partly lined with zinc, I saw another magic door. It opened to the outside of the house and the iceman could shove 100-pound blocks of ice through it into the icebox without ever coming into the house.

The basement was largely forbidden as a dangerous place. There was a boiler with an open gas flame, where all the whites (tablecloths, napkins, sheets, etc.) were boiled. There was also a coal bin—a small room where a child could become totally black—the big roaring furnace that scared me, and Dad's workbench. If he was working there some Saturday afternoon in winter, I might venture downstairs. If my brothers were there, he would tell them the names of the tools, and maybe let them pound a nail into a scrap board. I would just watch. Dad always wore a suit to work and to meetings. Only at the workbench or in the garden or later at the lake did I see him in an old open shirt and a pair of gray "work pants." He would sometimes hum in his melodious bass voice when his work was going well, but he could shout alarming swear words in that same deep voice when he was frustrated by a bent nail or a tool that wouldn't work. "Hell" and "damn" were the worst words I ever heard, but they were delivered with such fury that I would head immediately for the open wooden stairs to the kitchen.

On Monday, laundry day, I might watch mother at the wash machine, wringing clothes into the rinse tubs from the machine with the agitator, and hear warnings about not getting my hand in the wringer. On Tuesday, ironing day, she would stand at the gas-fired mangle, ironing all our sheets, pillowcases, and table linen, while the maid, when we had one, would use an ironing board for shirts, children's clothing, and mother's blouses and cotton housedresses.

During the summer, I avoided the kitchen. Mother and the maid would have huge kettles boiling on the stove, filling the place with steam while the temperature outside might be in the 80s or 90s. The smells were good because they were "putting up" canned peaches, pears, and applesauce. Sometimes when I walked through, I would see a cheesecloth jelly bag hanging on a broomstick with the red juice from currants or other berries slowly dripping into a bowl. That juice would eventually become jelly. Mother canned tomatoes, and, from the apples on our trees, she made apple butter and sliced apples for pie. We had a plum tree that yielded jam and jelly. Mother also made dill pickles and bread-and-butter pickles. In those days, some canned goods were available, but there was no frozen food and almost no prepared foods. We bought bread at the bakery, but the pies, cakes and cookies were all baked from scratch, usually on Friday, baking day. Food was much more seasonal than it is today. We had apples, oranges and bananas during the winter, but no other fruit. Homegrown vegetables like carrots, rutabagas, turnips, cabbage and potatoes were the most common in the winter. Strawberries and asparagus appeared in the spring, but briefly.

The playroom, or sunroom, was at the back of the main floor, connected to the dining room by French doors. I had my doll buggy there and a few dolls, always named Dorothy. I would rather play with the boys' blocks and trains because my brothers seemed to do such fascinating things with them. As long as George was home, we always played together in the sunroom or in the backyard, where there was a sandbox full of white sand. With his brown curly hair, his big smile, and his clever hands, he was more important to me than anyone else. We made cities in the sand. Sometimes I was allowed to take my kiddy car to the sidewalk in front of the house. George had a big red wagon and we would play we were delivery men. After we got swings in the backyard—big tall ones on frames made of metal pipes—plus rings and a bar for hanging by your knees, other neighborhood children came to play. This equipment, the only kind available, was meant for grade schools. It was a long time before I could swing, and the rings always eluded me.

I had to stay in the house or the backyard until the summer I was four; then I was allowed on the sidewalk anywhere on my block. Because I couldn't cross a street, I couldn't go to the empty lot with the older children, but I got acquainted with Susan who lived down the street to the left and Agnes, up the street past one house on the right. Betty lived in the duplex on the corner. Sometimes George would organize games for all of us, plus Jack (who lived in a duplex past Sue's house), Nathan, and one or two other boys. When we put on plays and puppet shows, the mothers who came paid us two pins for admission. I don't know what we did with those pins. The mothers knew each other and agreed on rules about children being home as soon as it got dark and not going off the block until we were in first grade. We had rules for crossing streets drilled into us. Agnes' family was Catholic, Susan's was Episcopalian, Jack's was Lutheran, Nathan's and ours were Jewish, but I was unaware of those differences until I was seven or eight.

I took my naps and slept in my little bedroom which had a dresser and a chair beside the bed. The window opened to a tiny porch where Mother or the maid could shake out rugs and the dust mop. When I got old enough I liked to crawl out there. My closet was up a high step because it was above the staircase.

In the summer, when I had to go to bed while it was still light outdoors, I listened to the murmur of adults talking on the front porch and to streetcars banging along Grand Avenue and wanted to get up. In the winter I slept under piles of Hudson Bay blankets in the freezing air from the open windows and thought only of burrowing deeper into my bed.

One morning in spring, I woke up and couldn't see. The world was red and black. I began to scream and somehow felt my way to my parents' room. Mother took me in her arms and carried me to the bathroom where she bathed my eyes until I could open them. The lids had stuck together with some discharge. I was still panicked and crying so she took me into her bed to snuggle and be comforted. It is one of the few times I remember ever being in her bed; and I know I was never in my father's bed. Their twin beds had high, dark mahogany head and footboards. I can remember my father carrying me when we were on a "hike" somewhere, but he was not one to caress or kiss his children.

When we had a maid, her room was in the attic so it, like the basement, was mostly forbidden territory. My brothers' bedrooms were on the front of the house and I didn't enter them too often either. I appeared in the living room whenever Mother had company. It was dark, with heavy drapes I could hide behind; there was an oriental rug, whose design included those red spots I always stepped over. There was a special upholstered chair I couldn't sit in because it belonged to Kiki, my brother George's "'maginary friend" and not to be trifled with. George could see him although no one else could. If you sat on Kiki, George would scream. After George started school, when I was three, I too had a "'maginary friend"—my sister Alice, who was twelve years old, walked with crutches, so that she needed my help, and was very smart. She read to me and told me stories. She would magically disappear when George got home from school, but she would come out of her hiding place—the window seat in the dining room—when he left. I couldn't open the window seat—the cover was too heavy—but I knew she could stay in there. She only came out when I was alone, so I'm not sure anyone else knew about her, but we all knew about Kiki.

I could go outside in the winter, but my sister Alice couldn't because it was too slippery for somebody with crutches. I could even help George make a snowman or a snow fort. When we came in, we put our mittens on the steam radiator in the dining room and listened to the hiss of melting snow and smelled the wet wool. We had to watch and turn the mittens so they wouldn't get hard from too much heat.

The winter I was four, Mother was president of the St. Paul chapter of the National Council of Jewish Women. By then my older brother, Linn, was nine and George was seven. Mother's desk with the black Bakelite telephone on it was in the corner of the playroom. Bakelite was the only plastic we had in our house at that time. The phone had a mouthpiece that looked like a horn which mother spoke into. She told "Central" what number she wanted. I was not to disturb Mother when she was talking on the phone, but I learned that if she was sitting quietly, she might put her hand over the mouthpiece and answer a question. On the other hand, if her legs were crossed and her foot was swinging, I had better not bother her. She would scold me for interrupting.

"Council" owned and operated Sophie Wirth Camp at White Bear Lake. This camp provided a vacation for mothers and children from the "West Side" and Capitol neighborhoods of St. Paul, where many poor Jewish immigrant families had settled, as well as for youngsters from observant families in other parts of the Twin Cities. At the time, it claimed to be "the only kosher camp in the northwest" which included Wisconsin and the Dakotas. From her days of public school teaching in Chicago and volunteering at Hull House, Mother was motivated and knowledgeable about helping others. As camp chairman, she managed the camp for many years.

Those preschool days went slowly for me, although my memories are compressed. Dad told us stories about a boy named Billy and his dog Copy, who tried to copy everything Billy did with comic results. They found a hollow tree and went down through the hollow roots to a magic underground kingdom. Mother read to us and I loved books long before I could read. I remained awkward and small for my age and kept on talking, and finally I reached the momentous age of five, when a new life began for me, both at school and in the family.

3

Five Years Old

I grabbed my jacket in the vestibule and ran outside to the backyard on the morning of my fifth birthday. May 5th, and snow on Daddy's tulips—some of the thick stems were arched over in defeat and some of the yellow and orange blossoms were standing up stiffly, snow in their little cups. Snow in May, I learned in subsequent years, was not a total rarity in Minnesota—it has snowed more than once on my birthday.

The world suddenly opened for me that day, when my brother George, then in second grade, told me that he was taking me to kindergarten because, he said, when you're five you can start school. I wasn't officially supposed to start until the following September. We walked the sidewalk that I knew well, then crossed the street and took the diagonal path across the empty lot to Summit Avenue where rich people lived in big houses. We walked along Summit—then paved with wooden blocks—to Fairview, across the green boulevard that divided Summit, and along Fairview to Grand Avenue where the stores were located and the streetcar tracks gleamed in the sun. We turned left on Grand for two blocks to Ramsey School, an old dark-red stone building. We went up the grooved steps and George presented me to tall and kindly Miss Van Dusen. She looked down at me and smiled and said if I behaved nicely I could stay until lunchtime. There were lots of children sitting at little low tables; I immediately had a revelation about drawing trees. George was very good at drawing, but I wasn't. The child next to me was carefully drawing a thick stem with a brown crayon, and then a round green ball on top of the stem with a green crayon. A tree! I copied it immediately and was very proud of my success.

We walked home, had peanut butter sandwiches at the kitchen table and told Mother all about it. She had talked with Miss Van Dusen on the telephone and had learned that I had behaved nicely and could come to morning kindergarten, for the rest of the term until June. That was a preview of my grade school career. After spending some six weeks in morning kindergarten I was promoted to afternoon kindergarten that fall. School, Mother told Dad, was my oyster. I wasn't sure what that meant, but I loved it from the beginning. I loved books and reading and playing with the other children at recess and especially being where my brothers were. I was old enough at last.

I told my mother I wanted to be a writer and write stories and poems. She was very encouraging; she bought me a notebook and wrote down my first efforts at dictation. Mother told me I was badly coordinated, but instead of helping me learn to use my hands and body, she reasoned that she should encourage my reading and studying. The kitchen was mostly out of bounds because I spilled things—or maybe cooking meals for six people was just more efficient without a little girl underfoot. I would hear, "Go read a book" or "Go out and play" and later, "Practice your piano" or "Have you done your homework?" Unfortunately for me, I believed her. I did not try to be athletic or to use my hands.

I hated gym. I was the smallest in the class and the least able to catch a ball or climb a rope. Gym class took place three days a week in the mildew-smelling basement of Ramsey School. Although the spare, dark-haired gym teacher with the commanding voice wore bloomers, the children didn't change their clothes. I was okay at marching to a record of Sousa's marches, but when it came to folk dancing, my left leg came up when I intended to raise my right. I wouldn't cry, I just went and stood by the wall and watched. I couldn't chin myself or catch a ball. The teacher looked at me and sighed, but she didn't make me try very often.

Now that I was going to school I was allowed to go across the street to the empty lot if George was going there too. The empty lot was the scene of a good deal of fort building, which meant digging holes, piling up branches and loose rocks to make walls and other endeavors that were seldom finished. There was one tree that some kids could climb. Not me. But somehow it was infinitely more interesting than the swings and bars in our backyard.

We didn't observe very many Jewish customs in our home. However, my father did some things that I didn't know until much later were customary. For example, he planted a tree for each child. My tree, a white pine, still towers over the garage behind the house where I grew up. He also told Mother to put apples and honey on the table at the Jewish New Year, Rosh

Hashanah. He said this custom was to wish us all a sweet new year. When we dipped the apples in the honey, they tasted wonderful. He insisted on washing his hands before every meal, and when we went to a restaurant, he always asked where to "wash up" before the meal. I don't know if he said or thought of the customary blessing for washing hands.

My mother didn't keep kosher, saying she didn't believe in "Culinary Judaism." For her, Judaism was both intellectual and a matter of trying to achieve social justice. She didn't observe or possibly even know about old Jewish customs.

My father liked to tell us Jewish stories. The first time I heard about the golem was when I was about five or six. My mother used to love to read and she didn't like to be disturbed. So one dreary Saturday afternoon, I asked her for something to do. Dad was down in the basement at his workbench, hammering away.

"Did you clean up your room?"

"Yah," I said.

"Yes, Mother," she said.

"Yes, Mother," I said, "I haven't got anything to do."

"Look out any window and draw something you see out there," she told me.

I went to the shelves in the sunroom where crayons and paper were kept, but somebody had put them on a high shelf. I tried and couldn't reach. Then I thought that if I jumped up, I could grab the crayon box. But when I tried, the whole shelf came tumbling down—with crayons and paper, a tin box of dominoes, another box of pencils all scattered around. Luckily I jumped out of the way, but it made a terrible noise. Mother came in, looked annoyed, and called my father.

"What happened?" he asked me, looking at the mess. I expected him to start yelling at me, but he didn't. I answered, "Mom told me to draw a picture and I was trying to get the crayons and the shelf fell down."

Dad started to laugh. It was always better when he laughed, but I never knew if he'd be mad or amused. "Are you a girl or a golem?" he asked me.

"What's a golem?"

"You pick up the stuff," he said, putting the shelf back up, "and then I'll tell you." So I handed him everything except the crayons and the dominoes which I had to put back in the boxes. When I finally finished, he sat down on the rocker and took me on his lap and told me the story of the golem. "This is a story my father told me," he began.

Once upon a time, more than four hundred years ago, a famous rabbi lived in the city of Prague. (In this city today, he said, I had a great uncle. If we ever went to Europe I would meet him, but this story happened a very long time ago.) The rabbi's name was Judah Loew and times then were bad for the Jews. They had to live in a ghetto with walls around it, and they could only leave for a few hours in the day. They were very poor and the count who ruled the city and the surrounding countryside was cruel to them.

Once a priest kidnapped a little Jewish girl named Rachel. He thought he would save her soul by converting her to Christianity. The count wouldn't help the Jewish parents get her back, so they went to Rabbi Loew for help. That night Rabbi Loew dreamed he should make a golem to help in this terrible time. He took two of his followers and they went down to the Moldau River late at night when there was no moon. It was very dark and they had only one lantern with them. First they made a very large man out of the clay by the river. Then the rabbi walked around him seven times saying magical prayers. Then each of the others walked around seven times, saying mystical words that the rabbi had taught them. First the clay man seemed to be on fire. Next he seemed to be wet and water ran out of his mouth. Then the rabbi wrote the secret name of God, which is never pronounced, on a piece of paper and put it in the clay man's mouth. The man took a deep breath and sat up. He looked at the rabbi.

"Your name is Joseph Golem," the rabbi told him. "You will do whatever I tell you to do to help the Jewish people. Now get up and come with me."

The golem was enormous, towering over the rabbi. But he was awkward—he had never learned to walk! The rabbi held the golem's hand as he tried to walk, stumbling and almost falling. As they went back toward the town, his walking got better. He didn't talk—in fact, he never could talk, because he wasn't human—but he could understand and obey.

The next day the rabbi gave him his first assignment: to bring back little Rachel, who had been taken by the priest and was now in a convent with a very high wall around it.

The rabbi told Joseph Golem exactly how to find the convent, to climb over the wall, to recognize Rachel and reassure her by patting her hand gently, and carry her back to the rabbi's house. No ordinary man could have hoisted himself over that wall and crossed the pieces of broken glass on the top. The golem could do it. He was so strong he had no trouble climbing over the wall and there he saw Rachel in a little garden. She was crying while two people talked to her. The golem simply picked her up. The people were so surprised and so frightened by his size that they did nothing. He patted her hand, carried her over the wall and back to the rabbi very quickly. His feet flew over the rough cobblestones of the streets in the ghetto. Rachel just barely had time to see that she was in the rabbi's house when her mother and father came to get her. Everyone was crying and laughing, hugging each other and thanking the rabbi all at once.

It seemed that the golem would be a wonderful help to the poor Jews in the ghetto, and indeed he was, as long as the rabbi gave him careful instructions. But once the rabbi's wife was busy preparing a Rosh Hashanah meal for a lot of people. She needed some apples. She saw Joseph Golem just standing there, so she told him, "Go to the market and get me some apples." So what do you think happened? Being very strong but not very smart, the golem went to the market, saw the woman sitting at her booth with apples, and simply picked her up, chair, booth, apples and all, and carried her, yelling and kicking, to the rabbi's house!

The rabbi's wife had to call the rabbi to get Joseph Golem to put the woman down, and after the rabbi had paid her, he had to tell the golem to take the booth and the chair back again. He must let the woman walk.

"Now, dear," the rabbi said, "remember he has to be told exactly what to do; but, in any case, he can only do what helps the Jewish people."

Just the same, a few years later, after the golem had been helpful in many difficult situations, the rabbi's son wanted to scrub the floor of the paved courtyard in front of their house. Since he was preparing for the Sabbath, he thought it would be okay to send the golem for water, and he told the golem to go to the river and bring water.

Then he went into the house to study until the golem came back, but soon he heard his mother saying, "Stop, stop!" and calling his father. The golem had brought one pailful after another until the courtyard became flooded and water poured into the kitchen. The rabbi finally came out of his study and stopped the golem, who didn't know that one bucketful was enough. You always had to tell him exactly what to do.

After my Dad told me these stories, he said, "Now don't be a golem. If somebody says 'Draw a picture,' do they have to tell you 'First go in the sunroom, then pull up a stool, then climb up and get the crayons and paper, then take them to the little table, sit down, and draw one picture and then stop?'" I shook my head.

"You're a girl," he told me. "You can talk and you can figure things out, so don't be a golem."

"Okay," I said, "but will you tell me some more stories some time?"

"Sure I will," Dad said.

During the summer I was five we rented a cottage at Bald Eagle Lake, while our place at Bone Lake was being built. My father's parents, Rosalie and Jacob Firestone, had a cottage at Bald Eagle. It was a little brown-and-white frame house with a big front porch facing the lake from a high bank; there was a big flower and vegetable garden in back. My father told us that before he was married, he worked downtown and took the train to the little Bald Eagle station. If he was late his brother Allan would leave a kerosene lantern for him in the station and he used it to walk home along the country roads.

My grandparents' cottage had a noisy pump in the backyard that gave them running water from their well. That was a
sad summer because my grandmother was dying. My father's
younger brother Allan, his wife Rose, and their two children
also rented a cottage to be near her, and my father's older sister
Estelle and her husband, Albert, came from Chicago to visit
with their son Bobby, my brother Linn's age. Rose and Allan's
children, Danny and Phyllis, were my cousins who lived on
Lincoln Avenue in St. Paul, only a few blocks from us. Every
year we had Passover with them. My toddler cousin Phyllis
had lovely golden curls which I envied then and for some time
afterwards.

Death doesn't mean much to a five year old. I had seen my
grandmother Rosalie working in her garden—she loved flowers and grew beautiful ones. I had seen her sitting on the porch
sewing. But now she was in bed and I was only taken to see her
once, when she tried to smile and didn't say much. Her life
ended before the summer was out, and my parents decided I
was too young to go to the funeral. My grandfather sold the
house on Goodrich and moved into the Angus Hotel at Selby
and Western. We went to visit him every Sunday after Religious School, which I entered the fall I was "going on" six. We
had Sunday dinner in the dining room and I decided that my
father must be very rich because the dinner cost one dollar per
person. The tables had white tablecloths and linen napkins,
and we were waited on by black men in tuxedoes who were
very kind to us children and very proper to the adults. The
dinner was soup, medium rare roast beef, baked potatoes,
canned peas, iceberg lettuce salad, soft rolls, and apple pie. It
was my favorite meal, so as I look back, I must have learned to

eat something. But there were some foods that still made me nauseated—especially fish, and oddly enough, cooked carrots. Mother had almost given up trying to get me to eat them.

My grandfather had been a joker and a storyteller, but when I climbed on his lap for a story in his hotel room, he said he couldn't tell any more stories now that grandma had died. I climbed down and went away.

One of his stories about his life in Szaled, Abany Torna, Hungary, went like this: As a little boy, Grandpa Jacob went to "Cheder" in the little town in Hungary where he grew up. Cheder means room, and in those days in Jewish communities, a man who perhaps couldn't get any better job would set aside a room in his house and teach little boys to read Hebrew. By the time my grandparents were born in Hungary in the mid-nineteenth century, Jews had become partially emancipated. They no longer had to live in ghettoes and some previously forbidden jobs were open to them. My grandparents had gone to regular schools and learned to read and write both German and Hungarian, but the boys also had to learn Hebrew.

The boys there were mischievous and the teacher was drowsy. He put his head on his desk and fell asleep, his long black beard draped over the desk. My grandpa had a pair of scissors—or perhaps he found them on the desk, and he stole up and cut off the end of his teacher's beard without waking him.

When the teacher awoke and stroked his beard—as was his habit—and saw all the boys suppressing giggles, he was enraged.

"Who did it?" he screamed. Of course no one would confess. He screamed threats and curses and then calmed down.

"All right," he said, "I'll find out. Everyone stand up." They did. He turned his back and took the broom in his hand. "I am making a special blessing," he announced, "a special magic blessing." He turned around with several broom straws in his hand. "Now," he said, "each one of you will put a straw in your mouth." He stuck the broom straws in the boys' mouths as he spoke. "And we will stand here," he said, "and the straw in the mouth of the guilty boy will begin to grow, and when it gets long enough I will know who cut my beard!"

The boys stood quietly. The teacher turned his back. The room was silent. My grandfather looked down his nose at the straw in his mouth, and saw two of them because he couldn't look at a straw in his mouth without looking cross-eyed. Probably the teacher was just fooling. But maybe he wasn't. Grandpa Jacob looked again. Sure enough, the straw was growing. What to do? Well, he had the solution—he would bite off a little of the piece in his mouth and suck it in. He kept crossing his eyes to look and he kept biting the straw and sucking it in. Now the teacher turned around. Jacob had the shortest straw. He grabbed Jacob by the ear. "Aha!" said he, "Now I know," and out came the broomstick, used again, as it often had been before, to hit a boy's backside.

4

Bone Lake

I was sitting alone in our blocky black 1920s Dodge while my father went into the farmhouse to talk to the man who was going to build our cabin. I was five years old. My father never bought a Ford because Henry Ford was an anti-Semite. I was looking up at a huge, glorious flaming maple tree, yellow sunlight coming through its scarlet leaves. I thought "This is so beautiful, I wish I could remember it always, but I probably won't, I'm too young," but to this day I can see the image of that tree.

The following summer our cabin was built, my favorite place for many years. It was basically a one-room cabin with a fireplace, alcoves for sleeping, a big screened front porch on the lake side, and a small kitchen. There was no running water or electricity. The pump was outside the kitchen door and the outhouse was outside the door away from the lake. In front of the outhouse Dad put a highway sign that read "Historic Site Ahead," a gift he requested from a friend who had supervised repair of the two-lane road that is now Highway 61.

Down a few steps from the cabin was a low area, wet in spring and loaded with wildflowers all year long. Beyond that was the boathouse, built of brown-and-white siding to look like a log house and to match the cabin. We had a dock, a place to build outdoor cooking fires, and a picnic bench by the beach.

Dad was always busy; he hung an old tire from an oak tree as a swing for us. He made himself a crude outdoor stand near the pump for shaving. He cut down dead trees for firewood and had plenty of logs to split. He found a swamp full of yellow lady's slippers and transplanted some to bloom around the cottage. He got acquainted with Mr. Jensen, who operated the general store in Milltown, and Dad was friendly to John Anderson, the farmer from whom he had bought the land for our cabin. We got to know the younger of the eleven farm kids who were still at home. Mother was busy, too, cooking, making beds, taking us on walks, supervising our swimming.

Each trip from St. Paul to the cabin was long but full of happy anticipation. After we passed Taylors Falls, the Wisconsin roads were all gravel. But when we arrived, we were in what for me was a beautiful wilderness. Bone Lake was surrounded by woods and a few subsistence farms, a very few summer places, and one small resort across the lake from us, called Calderwood. I fell in love with Bone Lake for many reasons, mainly because our family was together there. Dad and Mother weren't always leaving for work or for Temple or for the meetings they went to all week long. The boys weren't at school, taking music lessons, or at Boy Scouts or religious school or going to places where I wasn't allowed to follow. Instead, they were there with me.

The lake and the woods enchanted me. Through my grade-school years, Bone Lake was my Garden of Eden. We walked barefoot along the pebbly shore, looking for a rock slightly larger than the others, picking it up quickly. Just before the crayfish, exactly the color of the rock, startled and scuttled away, we grabbed him behind his miniature monster claws and watched him wiggle in our hands. We'd laugh and put him back in the clear water and watch him scoot under another rock.

At a muddy weedy place just past our beach, we could catch green frogs if we were quick enough to grasp them, too, right behind their front legs. They were wet and slippery and often got away. Sometimes Dad gave us a pail with a removable screen on top to plop them in; he would use them for bait when he went out at twilight for bass.

There were many schools of minnows—shiners—in the shallow water. Dad had a seine, a net about a yard high and four yards long. Linn would hold up one pole near the shore, while Dad would walk out into the deeper water with the other and make a semicircle. They'd bring in enough minnows for an afternoon of fishing for crappies. We'd throw back clams and snails or anything else caught in the net that we couldn't use. Sometimes there were baby mud turtles with orange designs on the bottom of their shells.

My brother George was an imaginative fun-loving creator of games and projects. I was his willing, obedient, adoring younger sister, ready to follow and take orders. Linn was more likely to be drafted to help Dad with his hundreds of projects, like grubbing out stumps, planting white pines, putting up martin houses or taking them down to be cleaned, painting the boathouse. Sometimes Linn teased us; he never seemed to like the lake as much as we did. George, too, had to help later on, but when we were very young, the two of us were often left to our own devices. We built whole towns in sand on one of the beaches. We were Indians in the woods or pirates in the rowboat (tied securely to the dock).

Sometimes we went to Anderson's farm, about a ten minute walk, through woods and past a field. With the youngest farm girl, Violet, we could jump in the prickly hay or play with kittens in the barn, which smelled of manure and new hay. We might go to the pasture with her and the shepherd dogs to get the cows for afternoon milking. Or we might race the goat, Lindy, around the barnyard. We helped Violet search for eggs in the barn and watched her slop the pigs. When we got old enough, we tried riding on the broad backs of the Belgian work horses and milking the cows. My hands weren't strong enough.

At the lake, my help was needed in the kitchen as I grew older. In town, I was not welcome—too clumsy, I was told. But at the lake I learned to pump water, and after it was heated on the stove and Mother had washed the dishes, I could dry them and put them on a shelf behind a curtain. They were plastic, red and yellow, and I couldn't break them. The dishes in town were "good china."

Mother would take me for walks in the woods; I felt very close to her then. She loved the flowers and trees and I believed she knew the name of every one. We crossed a little bridge over a ravine that ran with water in the spring, making a lovely tinkling sound, and then stepped along a little path into the deep woods of maple, oak, basswood. We looked for blood-root and hepatica in early spring, later violets and trillium, gradually exploring farther and farther. In the open spots were prairie plants like goldenrod and wild sunflowers, and closed blue gentians in the fall. I loved the bounty of the woods near

us and those wherever we went on expeditions. We picked strawberries, raspberries, blueberries and blackberries as the season
went on. Exploring the woods was a never-ending treasure hunt
for me.

In the high summer, there would be company, sometimes
other families with children, once even the family of my future
husband. When I was nine, I preferred playing with his older
sister, who tolerated me. Because of the long drive, the families
would stay overnight. The used upper berth from a train would
be pulled down, admired, and we would debate who got to
sleep in it. For the children, extra old army cots would be
brought out, made up with scratchy, khaki blankets from World
War I army surplus stores. Everything at the lake was old, rus-
tic, or second hand. We wore old clothes. Although little girls
were supposed to wear dresses in those days, and ladies wore
skirts, when my legs got all scratched up in the woods, Mother
cut down some of George's old pants for me. She wore some of
Dad's old slacks, without much alteration—she and Dad were
pretty much the same height. What a relief for me not to wear
skirts or a garter belt holding up wrinkly, white cotton stockings! How great not to be told to pull my skirt over my knees!
I could even try to climb a tree or swing high on the tire swing
without someone yelling "I see London, I see France, I see
Ruthie's underpants." Even my brothers were not immune from
repeating this chant, learned so early on the grade school play-
ground.

I loved the water. Mother held the back of my bathing suit
while I lay in the water on my tummy and she exhorted me to
kick and wave my arms. After a while she let go and I was
swimming. She and Dad swam the breaststroke with their heads

high out of the water. Sometimes to be funny when we had company, Dad wore his straw hat and smoked his pipe while swimming. When I was told to kick like a frog, I knew what Mother was asking me to do. We had some logs—peeled, painted, about four feet long—to float, hang on to, sit on and paddle a bit. We tried inner tubes but the valves scratched us. Later, Linn and George invented a surfboard—a board tied behind the outboard motorboat. It had a rope handle and, after the boat got up to speed, we could stand up on the board and by varying our weight from one side to the other, could swoop around behind the boat. This was long before they invented water skis at Lake Pepin. It was fun and safe—the boat didn't go very fast.

Fishing wasn't my favorite thing, but it was good to be out with everybody in the boat, bringing in crappies and throwing back the spiny perch. I learned to bait a hook, and could often remove it from the fish's mouth and put him on the stringer. Dad always told me to be a good sport and I tried. When I was nine or ten I even learned to help Mother clean fish. Maybe that was reality training, but it took me a long time to learn to like eating what I cleaned.

Our rowboat was large, painted white on the outside and brown on the inside. We had shiny brown kapok pillows that would float if you fell in or if the boat tipped, as it did, once. The outboard motor responded sporadically to the rope wound around the top and jerked to get the motor started. I learned to duck when that stinging rope shot out at me.

But when the motor worked, the lake was ours. We could go to Calderwood, and could look at the beautiful spring where the watercress grew, or visit Mr. Calder in his stone and log lodge and ride his white pony, Snowball, or even have supper at his restaurant. We could visit the two big islands where we looked for bones from the Indian battles supposedly fought there.

At our cabin, the porch where we slept was screened on three sides, with canvas shades that had been waterproofed with some kind of tar or creosote. They could be raised by ropes if it rained. When we went to sleep out there, we heard the noises of frogs in the spring and katydids in the summer, sometimes little sounds of creatures running in the woods, tree branches moving in the wind. We smelled the clean, sharp, tarry smell of the shades as well as the fresh breeze coming from the lake. We could lie there and look at the stars blinking in the deep sky. Sometimes an owl would hoot. Sometimes on a warm night when the cows were turned out to pasture, we would hear them mooing far away.

When we first moved to our cabin, there was a little white wooden church nearby on a county road. It was a Catholic church and the priest, Father Gordon, was an American In-dian, as were most members of his congregation. The farmers around there mostly went to the Lutheran church. My parents invited Father Gordon over and he told us about the Indian battles that had taken place on the islands in our lake, and about the trading post by the outlet. The outlet was a little creek that ran into the Apple River, which ran into the St. Croix, which then joined the Mississippi. The French voyageurs would come and bring axes, knives, needles, glass beads, and other things the Indians liked and would trade with them for furs, like beaver or fox. That was all a long time ago. But we knew there was still an Indian village over on Pine Lake. Dad once asked Father Gordon what our name, Firestone, would be in the Chippewa language. He said, "Ish-Koo-Day-Hasin." Dad said it sounded like Hebrew, because 'ish' means man.

At the full moon in October (Dad called it the Harvest Moon), the Indians danced in a clearing by the outlet. We would lie in our cots on the porch, seeing the silver light come in around the shades. We would listen to the tom-toms, or drums, and they seemed to go all night, deep throbbing booms. When we were older, we went to watch the dances. My brother George joined the men and boys in the middle, and I even joined what was called the squaw dance in the circle outside the men. We just swayed sideways in little rhythmic steps but the men and boys jumped and bent over and turned and were very agile.

One day Mother said there should be a place for kids to get dressed and undressed for swimming so the cabin wouldn't get so full of sand from the beach. My father said he'd go to the Indian village and get one of the men to build us an Indian-style house.

"A tepee?" asked my biggest brother.

"No," said Dad. "The Indians around here didn't make te-pees. They made little round houses, called wigwams. They are woodland Indians. It's the Indians who live on the prairie who made tepees." Then he drew pictures to show us the difference.

Dad and the boys and I got in the car to go to Pine Lake to the Indian village. A rough muddy track led to the village which stood by a small lake. There was a big round wooden house where the Indians had dances in the winter. Otherwise there were a few houses made of wood, wigwams covered with tar paper, and a lot of wrecked cars. Men were standing by the lake fishing with long poles, so Dad went up to a man who wore overalls like all the farmers. Dad asked him if he would come and build a house for us. The man didn't answer. Then Dad said he'd pay him for the work and the material. The man started laughing. Then he said, "Building houses is women's work. Go ask my wife over there." He sort of pointed with his chin toward a woman squatting on the ground cleaning a fish. A cat was trying to eat the fish, too, and the woman was having trouble getting the cat away. She called out, "Peter," and a boy about my age came running. She just nodded her head toward the cat and he grabbed it and ran away.

My father came up to her and asked if she could build us a house like one of those, and he pointed at a wigwam.

"Okay," she said, "I'll come tomorrow," and went right on cleaning the fish. So we walked back to our car and drove away.

That night when we were having supper we talked about it. "Will she really come? Will she bring the little boy, Peter? Would he play with us?"

Two ladies appeared in the morning, carrying big sacks. Peter came, too. Dad showed them where he wanted the wigwam and they nodded. A few minutes later, they had disappeared. Where had they gone? After a while they came back with bundles of long basswood sticks from which they stripped the bark with their knives. They set the sticks in the ground in a circle, then bent the tops down and tied them together with the bark they had stripped off. It took quite a while, but after a long morning, they had built the whole framework for a little round house.

When my Mother offered them some lunch they took a blanket out of their bags, put away their knives, and sat down on the ground. Mother brought out hamburgers, potatoes, peas and some carrot sticks. She was always telling us to eat raw vegetables. We were eating the same thing inside the cabin. When Mother went out again all the food was gone, so she brought out more of everything. She thought they must be very hungry. Of course, as she had told us so often, she believed that you must feed the hungry. She thought maybe the Indians hadn't had any breakfast, so she fried up a lot more potatoes and meat and brought it to them. When Dad went out to talk to them the third portion was all gone, too.

The woman said to him, "Where's the tar paper?" He hadn't known he was supposed to get tar paper, but they said there wasn't enough birch bark any more. So Dad went into town to get the tarpaper and my brothers and Peter and I tossed a ball around. Peter didn't say anything, so we didn't know if he was having fun or not. After the women finished the wigwam, Dad paid them and the three just disappeared again. We thought they must have a secret trail through the woods to their village.

The next time Father Gordon came to visit us, Mom told him how the food had been gobbled up so fast. It was his turn to laugh. "You see," he explained, "for us it is rude not to finish what is set before us, so if they couldn't eat it all, they would have put it in their sacks to take home. They were being polite and showing that they appreciated what you were giving them. Not to eat it would have been insulting—telling you you weren't a good cook."

Afterwards, I wondered why she invited Father Gordon in but hadn't invited the others into the cabin to eat with us. Children are quick to notice inconsistencies.

Mother laughed. "It was good food," she said, "I hope they shared it with some hungry people, and it's fine that they got to laugh at us for not knowing about good manners."

Every year in the fall, right after Yom Kippur, the Jewish Day of Atonement (usually in September; it follows the new year, or Rosh Hashanah, by 10 days), we went to Bone Lake on a special mission to find bittersweet for decorating our house in town all winter and to pick mushrooms. Mother could identify redtop mushrooms, shaggymanes and puffballs, but the best were the brown oak mushrooms clustered around the oak trees and stumps in the Andersons' pasture. Mother then made wonderful fragrant soup and delicious dishes like buttery mushroom omelets. We scrambled through the pasture with sharp jackknives and brown paper bags or baskets. One year we saw a ghostly Indian pipe; every year we looked in that spot again but it never came back.

Mother always had a basket for every purpose. Dad came along and helped, but he kept an eye out for curious fallen branches or the roots of fallen trees. He collected these and when he got back to the cabin, he carved an elfin face or some strange animal. He lined up his carvings on a shelf; they made me laugh.

After we returned to the cabin, my job was to go outdoors with the cut pieces of the bittersweet vine. I carefully removed the pale green leaves, gathered the pieces of the vines with the berries, still in their pale orange-green shells, into small bunches. Then I tied the bottoms of the stems together with twine, making a loop so that someone taller could hang them in the house to dry. After a few days the shells opened like four flower petals, and the bright orange berries could be seen. In another few days they also dried, and the bunches could be arranged in vases to last all winter in our house in town. The twisting vines were like growing things and the berries like samples of sun-light to brighten our darkening days.

Like the mingled joys and sorrows of being Jewish, the fall expeditions were fun when we found the treasures of woods and pasture, but sad when we realized that summer was gone and school and serious city life were beginning again.

5

Jacob and Rosalie Firestone

In later years I learned the story of my father's parents, which began when my grandfather came to America.

The Jews of Jacob Firestone's village decided to send my grandfather to a school (a yeshiva) to become a rabbi. While in this larger town he hid books about science and new Western ideas in his Talmud folios. He read about the enlightenment (Haskala) in Hebrew and made his decision. At the age of nineteen, in about 1868, he ran away to America and went directly to Cleveland, Ohio, then a frontier town with many German-speaking people. Possibly he knew someone there; at any rate, he soon fell in love with a woman from his home territory, Esther Guttman (later changed to Goodman). But before he could marry her, he had to earn a living. He carried a backpack and went peddling to farms around Cleveland, bringing needles and thread, cloth, small tools, items needed on isolated farms far from towns and villages. He slept in barns where he traded and sold his items to the farmers. Peddlers carried news and told stories to lonely families, so they were usually welcome.

Many farmers spoke German and my grandfather soon began to learn English. He was five feet tall, with dark eyes, curly black hair and a grand mustache. My father said that carrying the pack had made him short. Others said he'd been born prematurely and hadn't grown. He had been fed with an eye-dropper, they said. And he could tell good stories. One time when the circuit riding pastor of the Lutheran church in the country failed to show up, my grandfather preached. He gave a sermon in German from his knowledge of the Hebrew Bible and was invited to stay on as pastor. He declined.

In due course he acquired a horse and wagon, but his progress as a capitalist was uneven. He had bought a whole wagonload of turkeys in the country to sell in Cleveland for Thanksgiving. But the horses bolted, spilling the cages, and the live birds all escaped. Back to peddling with a backpack!

Esther Goodman, meanwhile, had spurned him and married Michael Frankel. Her marriage was a blow to grandfather, and he wanted to leave Cleveland. He learned that James J. Hill was building a railroad west from St. Paul. The city had grown as the head of navigation on the Mississippi; large boats could not get farther upstream because of St. Anthony Falls. Jacob decided to go to St. Paul about 1873, where he found an opportunity to deal in scrap iron that the railway discarded while building tracks. Eventually he had a small warehouse on First Street by the river, where he dealt in secondhand goods of various kinds, and sometimes traded with Indians for furs. Three times the uninsured frame building where he kept his stock burned down. There were good years and years of economic panic. But toward the end of the 1870s he felt firmly enough established to write home and ask his parents to find him a bride. He would pay her passage money to America and meet her in New York, and if they weren't suited to each other, he wouldn't ask for the money back.

One day, just as he opened a letter from home and picked up the picture of a pretty young woman that fell out, Sol Goodman walked into his office and looked over his shoulder. Sol was Esther's brother.

"What are you doing with a picture of my little sister?" he asked

"That's not your sister—it's a girl my parents think might make a good wife for me," said Jacob.

"Well, what's her name? She's a dead ringer for my sister."

Jacob turned the picture over. The name Rosalie Guttman was written on the back. "I'm sending for her!" Jacob announced immediately.

My grandmother was a mail-order bride, eleven years younger than her groom, said to be beautiful, with curly red-gold hair and a lovely figure.

Rosalie came, they met, they married. Their proper Jewish wedding (I have the ketubah, or wedding contract) took place in Cleveland, perhaps at Esther's house, in 1882. They bought a Victorian house at 724 E. Seventh Street on Dayton's Bluff in St. Paul, facing a little triangular park. 'Stelle was born in 1884, my father Milton in 1886, and Allan in 1894.

My grandfather was such an upstanding citizen (and a naturalized citizen by then) that he was appointed to keep the key to the firebox on the corner. If someone wanted to call the fire department, he had to state his case to my grandfather before the call could go in to the horse-drawn fire engines at the nearby station. That way, no drunks or irresponsible kids could make the call just for the excitement.

Somewhere along the line, my grandfather began to buy rental property in St. Paul and attained financial security. The marriage was a good one, although I was told by more than one person that Rosalie was bright but very serious and often didn't understand Jacob's jokes and high jinks. Jacob was apparently always an optimistic, good-natured, risk-taking person.

A friend told me he once encountered Jacob with his grown sons, Allan and Milton, on the train.

"You're smiling," he said to Jacob, "and humming a little song and your sons look so sad."

"Well," Jacob retorted, "they have to put up with this funny old foreign father, but I've got these two wonderful, well-educated American sons!"

In fact, my feeling is that my grandparents led their children to Americanize as fast as possible; by the time the children were born Jacob had been in the country several years. Rosalie studied English, learned to drive a car in due time, and to play bridge. One of her cars was an electric that worked on batteries. They joined Mt. Zion Temple, which was Reform (liberal), and whose members were mostly German Jews. My grandfather served as treasurer of the congregation. My grandparents sent their children to high school and for more education after that.

They did something very uncharacteristic of Jewish parents: they sent my uncle Allan to a military school, St. John's in Wisconsin. As a result, he became an officer in World War I. They had decided to send him there because they thought he was too much of a baby. After my Aunt 'Stelle finished high school, she went to a music conservatory in Chicago to continue her piano studies. My father went to the University of Minnesota for two or three years. Since my grandparents didn't consider the local law school very good, he went to Northwestern University Law School in Chicago. He was on the editorial board of the first *Illinois Law Review*, published by Northwestern and University of Illinois law schools. He started his law practice in St. Paul about 1908.

When I was five, I felt the sadness in the house after my grandmother died. My grandfather lived on, ill and old, less than two years. He still had spunk: when Esther Goodman became a widow and moved to St. Paul he proposed to her when they were both in their seventies. She turned him down again!

One dark winter Sunday afternoon when I was about six, my father decided to teach my brothers to play chess. Even for him, it was too cold for one of our outdoor excursions to Battle Creek Park or the woods on the way to Stillwater. I thought chess was a game for men only, but that didn't stop me from pouting and starting to sob. My grandfather took me on his lap where he was sitting in his special little green easy chair. I rubbed my cheek against his rough whiskers and listened to his whispery old voice. To quiet me, he told me a Jewish legend about chess and the Jewish pope.

Once upon a time, back in the Middle Ages, Christians considered all non-Christians to be damned. Thus, Jews and Moslems and any other unbelievers were destined to go to hell. It seemed that there was a Jewish family in a German city who had a very bright little son. Since the mother and the father both worked hard to make enough money to live on, they employed a young Christian girl to take care of the little boy. This little boy learned to read and write when he was very young, much to the astonishment of the girl. Very few non-Jews learned how to read and write in those days. It wasn't necessary if you were a peasant, a soldier, or a craftsman who belonged to a shoemaker's guild or a textile worker's guild. Jews, on the other hand, tried to teach all their sons to read so that they could study the holy writings. Even though his father didn't have much time for him, this little boy had learned very quickly.

In the evening in the ghetto in their little dark house, the father, Joseph, taught the boy how to play chess. By the time he was four years old, the child could beat his father, except when Joseph employed a very unusual set of moves in the endgame. But soon the little boy had mastered even this set of moves.

One day, to their horror, when Joseph and his wife came home from work, the boy and the Christian girl were both gone. The gates to the ghetto had been locked for the night, so they could only search inside and soon they discovered that their child was not anywhere in the ghetto. They couldn't search outside until the next day when they went to the countryside where the girl's family lived. They knew nothing about their daughter or the little boy. The little boy's parents were distraught; it was not unusual for a Christian to want to save a Jewish child by taking him or her to be baptized. They consoled themselves by thinking that the girl had taken the boy to some church and would return with him soon. They realized that she liked the little boy very much and was somewhat in awe of his intelligence.

Days went by and the child and his nursemaid never reappeared. Joseph mourned as if the child were dead. They recited Kaddish. Many in the community sympathized with them.

Meanwhile, the girl had taken the little boy to a Jesuit monastery. She told the monks and priests how bright he was and when they asked him questions he had replied cheerfully. The Jesuits recognized that this four year old was indeed a genius. They told the girl she had done a very good deed to rescue this child for service to the church. They were kind to the boy and immediately began to indoctrinate him with their ideas and beliefs. He knew that he came from a Jewish family, but there was no way he could leave the monastery or find his way back. Even if he cried often at night in his little cell, he did not hate his new life because he was treated kindly. He soon accepted religious orders and grew up to be a leader in this monastery. As a young man, he was promoted from the priesthood to eventually become a bishop.

After many years a new duke and a new archbishop ruled the city where this little boy's family still lived. Joseph had become a leader of the Jewish people in the ghetto. When new taxes and new restrictive rules were made against the Jewish people, Joseph felt that many of them would be reduced to starvation. He pleaded with the duke and the archbishop but neither would listen. He felt that the archbishop must be the person who was more influential, and therefore he decided to undertake the long journey to Rome. He had heard that the present pope was not unkind to the Jews, and hoped that the pope might influence the German archbishop.

After many days' journey, mostly on foot, with stops overnight in ghettos where he stayed with fellow Jews, Joseph finally arrived at the ghetto in Rome. Jews there told him that the pope was considered brilliant and somewhat eccentric. They really didn't encourage him, but he decided he would try anyway. He got up early in the morning and walked to Vatican City where the Swiss guards stopped him. He had prepared a letter asking for an audience with the pope. The guards took the letter and left him standing for several hours. Finally a priest came and told him the pope would consider his application and that he should return in three days. He had very little money left, but the Jews in the Roman ghetto let him stay with them while he waited impatiently. Finally, he returned to Vatican City and was told that the pope would see him but only for ten minutes.

Joseph was taken through many halls and grand rooms, past beautiful sculptures and paintings, through dark passageways and a brilliantly lit large hall until he was brought to the pope's door. His guide told him he was being received in the pope's own residence. The guide was clearly astonished that the pope would even consider talking with this lowly Jew. Joseph entered and found himself face-to-face with a tall, handsome man wearing beautiful scarlet robes. The man lazily extended his hand expecting the Jew to kiss his ring. Joseph did so, although he didn't want to.

"And why are you here?" demanded the pope.

Joseph explained that his community was being persecuted by the duke and the archbishop and that he hoped this pope would help him.

The pope had a kind of a gleam in his eye. He said, "Is it true that the Jews are very good chess players?"

Joseph answered, "Yes, some of us do play chess."

The pope said that he would play a game with Joseph; if

Joseph won, the pope would write a letter to the archbishop ordering him to reduce the penalties he had created for the Jews. If he, the pope, won, he would not change the rulings.

Joseph was nervous while a servant brought in a table and set up a very beautiful carved ivory chess set. They began to play cautiously and Joseph saw that the pope was a good but not remarkable player. Joseph had more men remaining on the board and was beginning to feel confident that after all he would win his bet. The play continued until they got to the endgame. Now Joseph was really feeling sure of himself, when suddenly the pope began to make all of the moves of Joseph's own secret way to win. In fact, the pope made the moves so quickly that Joseph had lost the game almost before he realized it. He jumped from his chair, looked again into the young pope's face, and exclaimed, "You are my son! The only person in the world who knows these moves except me is my son. I taught it to you when you were four years old."

The pope rose in his great red robes and embraced the old bearded Jew. He said, "For years I have been playing chess with Jews from German towns, hoping against hope that I would find my father."

Needless to say, the archbishop received his new orders from the pope and Joseph went home a happy man. I even believe he was able to bring his wife to Rome to see her son.

My grandfather and my father were great storytellers—to distract a child, to teach a lesson—and somehow they always told a Jewish tale. Mother was more apt to read to us from new books.

As I grew older, I understood my grandparents had not only been concerned with their grandchildren and their own children but also with many others. My father used to tell us that although he had a bedroom of his own when he was a boy, he seldom got to sleep in it. That was because his parents' home in St. Paul had been a way station, a place to stop, for relatives arriving from Europe. The relatives came for maybe a month, maybe a year. He and his brother had to give up their bedrooms and sleep in the living room.

My father wanted to be an orator and he was on the debate team—both in high school and at the University of Minnesota. When he told me about this, he began to chuckle. He said he would practice his speeches in front of the mirror in the living room when he wasn't able to use his own room. The result was that one set of relatives thought he was insane because he was talking to himself and they moved out rather quickly. He tried it on the next set, but it didn't work.

Besides the families that came, my mother told me the story of my father's first cousin, Minnie Firestone. Minnie's parents did not want to come to the United States, but they decided to send her. When she was nine years old, she left her home in Hungary, then still part of the Austrian Empire, and went with a neighboring family to Hamburg. There they boarded a ship for the United States; they traveled in steerage. Like many Jewish travelers from Orthodox homes, Minnie was not supposed to eat any food prepared on the ship. She carried hard-boiled eggs, dried bread, and a few other kinds of foods that required no refrigeration. I am sure she was very hungry when she got to Ellis Island. Steamships in the latter part of the nineteenth century took about ten days to get to New York from Europe. Minnie passed the various physical and mental exams given amidst the mobs of immigrants, although it must have been a very frightening experience for a nine-year-old child who didn't know any English. At any rate, the officials gave her a tag that said, "Minnie Firestone. Send to Jacob Firestone, St. Paul, Minnesota." The story handed down in the family is that the Black porters on the railroad trains were very kind to her and ultimately, after about three days on the trains, she was delivered to my grandfather at his warehouse by one of these men. They knew him well because he shipped used paper east for recycling so frequently that he had a free pass on the railroad. I was told that most of the Black people who lived in St. Paul at that time were employed on the railroads. The railroads offered what were considered good jobs and the Blacks that had them were seen as middle-class people, although real estate practices forced them to cluster in the Rondo Street neighborhood.

Minnie remained with my father's family while other immigrants came and went. She learned English, went to school, and helped my grandmother in the house. She was older than my father. When she was about nineteen, she met and married Joe Levy, a man who had become wealthy in the furniture business. She married him after his first wife died, helped raise his children and had some of her own. When I was young, I was in awe of my cousins who lived in a big, luxurious, yellow brick house on the River Road.

My mother's strong belief and practice that Jews must help each other and that those with privileges must help the less privileged, no matter who they were, was not original with her. Obviously, my father's parents, with their house like a Noah's Ark, had behaved the same way. Growing up as I did in a middle-class Jewish family did not prevent me from sharing experiences of people from many other places and situations. I was indoctrinated with the idea of my obligations to others, which has not left me.

I wish I had known my gutsy, risk-taking, generous immigrant grandparents who had the drive to educate their children, but I was a little over six when my grandfather died. His special stories and his individual sense of fun died with him.

6

At Sixes and Sevens in St. Paul

My mother was Jewish, but she wasn't a Jewish mother. She was neither over-protective nor over-indulgent. Because of her own mother's early death, she hadn't received much mothering herself. After she finished Vassar College, she taught elementary school in Chicago. The children, mostly Black and newly-arrived from the South, had never seen plumbing or electricity, which she had to teach them how to use. She had forty or forty-five children in a classroom, and she particularly enjoyed folk dancing with them, but she also taught them to read, realizing what children needed to know to succeed in school. She said that teaching was mostly social work, similar to her volunteering at Hull House when Jane Addams was there. Irma was a very independent person herself, and wanted us to be independent.

One morning when I was in first grade, she put a streetcar token in the pocket of my dress and secured it with a safety pin. She instructed me to take the Grand Avenue streetcar downtown after school and to meet her at the children's room in the public library. I wasn't afraid of the streetcar, and I knew where to get off, by the big white building facing Rice Park. What frightened me, but of course I wouldn't tell her, was the children's librarian, Miss McGregor. Although I knew she was a friend of my mother's, I was convinced that she must be Farmer McGregor's daughter, and that if I said the wrong thing, she might put a flower pot over my head.

After school I crossed the street with the police boy, a sixth grader with a big red flag, and got myself on the yellow streetcar, which I had often taken with my mother. At that point I felt quite grown up until a woman with a black hat sat next to me and said, "Aren't you the little Firestone girl?" I nodded. She gabbed on, "Your father is such a fine man and does so much for our temple, and your mother is wonderful, too. I know her in Council, of course." That was Council of Jewish Women.

Instead of standing on the yellow cane seat to ring the bell for my stop, an exercise I enjoyed, this woman in the black hat would ring it for me. I got off and marched through the basement door to the children's room. My mother wasn't there, and tall Miss McGregor loomed over me. "What book would you like?" she asked. I was so dumbfounded I said, "Peter Rabbit?" and she smiled and said I was really too old for that. She brought me something else, and I sat at the little table, feeling my cheeks get red until Mother finally arrived.

Most of the time when I was six or seven I was busy with public school or playing with the kids on the block. There were three girls my age. Agnes went to St. Mark's parochial school. I knew the teachers were nuns who wore black robes and were very strict. The other two girls were Protestant and went to public school like me. The fact that one, Susan, was adopted was far more intriguing to me than her religion. In the next block was a girl my age, Micky, who was Jewish and in my Sunday school class.

I started religious school on Sunday mornings when I was six. It seemed quite natural to us to think of the stories of Abraham, Isaac, Jacob, and Joseph as if they were about our own family. My brothers sometimes looked at me with disgust and said I was the favorite. At least they wouldn't throw me down a well the way Joseph's brothers did, would they?

My father was a mysterious person to me in those years, and afterwards, too. He never discussed his religious feelings or beliefs with us children, and yet I knew being Jewish was very important to him. Did God talk to my father the way He talked to Abraham? My father was always so absolutely sure he was right about so many things. Did God tell him? My parents went to temple every Friday night yet somehow I knew it was more important to my father than it was to my mother.

I knew he was a lawyer, but I wasn't allowed to go to his office and what he did there was another mystery. Every night after dinner Dad would lie down on the couch and put a newspaper over his head. He said it was to "snooze." Did he really sleep? Suddenly the paper would erupt like a small volcano, and he would be on his feet, on his way to some meeting, his watch chain dangling from his vest. He didn't have to comb his hair; he was bald. Wednesday nights it was lodge meeting; I knew he was a thirty-third degree Mason and master of his lodge, but this was a real mystery. Mother told me it was all secret and even she didn't know what they did, but these were high honors. Why was it so important? I wasn't supposed to bother my father with questions and I didn't, not because Mother said so, but because of the final and most difficult mystery of all: mostly, if we asked a question, he laughed and sat down and told us the answer in a loving tone of voice. But sometimes he got angry and yelled at us in a big bass voice that was really frightening. As a child, I couldn't anticipate his moods—and he was always dramatic about expressing them. I learned to be silent.

When I was six or seven, my Jewish father was not the only person who puzzled me. My Jewish friend, Micky, like some of the others, had a mother who spoke with a trace of foreign accent. And I could hardly understand her grandmother at all. As I met other grandmothers, they all seemed to speak with foreign accents, wear aprons, and make a lot of cookies with Yiddish names.

My mother's stepmother, Donny, had gone back to Chicago to live at the Hyde Park Hotel near Lake Michigan. She was still small, neat, and proper, her short, white hair always carefully arranged. She came to visit us in the summer, sometimes staying at the Lowry Hotel, sometimes staying at Calderwood during the week until we came up to Bone Lake on the weekend and took a boat ride to bring her back with us. She made me beautiful things, like elegant little dresses for my dolls. What I liked best were the costumes she made for me to wear out of Denison's crepe paper. I could be a pink rose with green leaves, or a Dutch girl with a blue dress and a white apron and cap with wings. She also made beautiful needlepoint seats for my mother's new dining room chairs; they were many colors blended together in an art deco diamond design she had created herself. But she didn't bake cookies and she didn't speak with an accent like Micky's grandma and some of the others I had met. So one day I asked her if she was Jewish.

Donny was very annoyed. "Of course I'm Jewish. What on earth made you think I'm not? Your whole family is Jewish as far back as we know—probably all the way back to David and Abraham. Why did you ask me?"

My stomach was dropping into my shoes, but I was too young to dissemble. "All my friends that are Jewish—their grandmas talk with funny accents and they make cookies all the time, and they don't do needlepoint."

Now she could laugh. "I was born in America, darling, just like your mother and dad. My grandparents came from Germany a long time ago—so did a lot of Jewish people—but other Jews came from other parts of Europe more recently because things were so hard for them in places like Russia and Poland. Some of them were poor and your parents tried to help them." She looked down at her canvas and poked her needle into exactly the right spot.

I learned early that they—the Christians—had Christmas, but we had Passover. I saw the Christmas trees in my friends' houses and I wished we could have one, but I don't remember any discussion. It simply wasn't done. Chanuka in my childhood was not much of a holiday and no one seemed to think of building it up to counteract what went on in school, the shops, everywhere in December. Nevertheless, sometimes during Christmas vacation, we would drive up and down Summit Avenue to look at the pretty lights on people's houses, and my father would start us singing "Ein Keloheinu," a Hebrew hymn to the glory of God, often sung after Sabbath services. We bellowed out the Hebrew song while we looked at the Christmas lights, an ambivalent joke.

I also learned that some people didn't like Jews, but in my early childhood, I was told that anti-Semitism was declining. Just the same, in my second-grade room there was a boy named Peter. When I walked down the aisle to go to the blackboard, he stuck his foot out, hoping to trip me. It slowed me down enough to hear him whispering, "Dirty Jew, you're a dirty Jew." In spite of Peter, whose little blue eyes and pug nose made me decide he looked like a pig, I absorbed some of the stereotypes about Jews. I thought, for example, that all Jews were short and dark, like me, even though my cousin Phyllis and many of the Jewish people I knew were blonde, redheaded, or tall.

Being Jewish wasn't a serious matter for me when I was six and seven. Most of the time I did what other children my age were doing at school or while playing outdoors on the block. I liked horses, for example, and like other children learned to stay away from their hind legs so I wouldn't get kicked. In town and on the farm, I sometimes could pet their soft velvet noses or give them a sugar lump and feel their rough huge tongues lick my hand.

The milkman, the iceman, and the vegetable man drove horse-drawn wagons in those days. They came along the street, but the ragman, who collected old rags, used clothes, bottles, and even furniture, came down the alley with his poor old nag. I don't know if he was a Jew, but we thought so—another stereotype. The milkman, whose horse was trained to walk to the next house and stop, spoke with a Scandinavian lilt like Mrs. Hasslen, my friend's mother. She called her son *Yack* instead of Jack, and we thought that was funny. The vegetable man, Tony, was Italian and he came only in the summer. But the giant ice man with the black rubber cape came all year round. I was a little afraid of him; he looked as if he could sling one of us over his shoulder; we didn't weigh as much as those one hundred-pound blocks of ice.

In the summer we were usually home during the week and at Bone Lake on weekends. When the ice wagon came up the street, while the giant was loping around to the back of the house to put the huge block of ice through the special little door that led directly to the icebox, we liked to try to find little ice chips in the sawdust on the bottom of his wagon. We'd brush the sawdust off and suck on the wonderful cold chips, even as they melted in our hands.

Mostly the iceman ignored us, but once when my brother and I had climbed partway up on the wagon to find more chips, he clucked to his horse and we found ourselves galloping down the street. I was half on and half off. If I had pulled up, I would have gotten slivers in my stomach. He stopped suddenly, and I lurched off the wagon. I wasn't hurt but scared and out of breath. George jumped down immediately. The iceman turned around, glared, and said, "And don't climb on my wagon again!" I don't think we ever told our parents about that particular scary adventure, unable to guess if Dad would guffaw or yell at us.

We played hide-and-go-seek with the kids on our block, ran through the hose in our bathing suits when it was hot, rode around on trikes and wagons and scooters, made forts in the empty lot and tried not to get scolded for being dirty. We had a few jobs, too, picking up the windfalls from the three apple trees in the yard, weeding the vegetable garden, going to the store for Mother. If we ever said we didn't have anything to do, she was ingenious in finding work for us. It was a fine way to teach us to amuse ourselves.

When I was growing up the only immunizations were for small pox and diphtheria-tetanus. Because of the fear of tuberculosis, we slept under many Hudson Bay blankets with windows wide open all winter long. Many families slept on unheated sleeping porches, even in the winter. Lots of fresh air was considered a cure or prevention for tuberculosis before the days of antibiotics. Mother had visited some Jewish children who were tuberculosis patients at the children's sanitarium at Lake Johanna, north of St. Paul. She told me how the children went outside in the winter with only thin clothing—boots, mittens, and hats—but no coats or warm jackets. I was very happy I was healthy and didn't have to do that.

Nevertheless, by the time I was six, I had had mumps, measles, and chickenpox, courtesy of my brothers, who brought these children's diseases home. Seasons for these diseases were well-known in the schools and homes; measles usually erupted after the Shrine Circus in the spring. When we had these outbreaks, a man from the Health Department came and nailed big yellow signs on the front door, the back door and even the side door. Those were quarantine signs. They told any visitor the diagnosis of the inmates. No one was supposed to enter or leave the house unless he or she had already had that disease. When we were sick, and even when we were beginning to feel fine, we had to stay in the house a prescribed number of days. If I were well but a brother had a children's disease I had never had, I must stay in the house. This was simply considered a normal part of growing up. I didn't have whooping cough until I was a little older and my friend, Betty, who lived two houses down the block, had it at the same time. To my surprise and joy, Mother permitted me to run down the alley to Betty's house if I promised not to breathe on anybody. It was a little like getting out of jail.

The most frightening illness that beset our family was when my brother George got scarlet fever. He was very ill and I knew without being told that he might die. Other children had died of scarlet fever. I was very frightened because I couldn't imagine life without him. I needed him to play with, and yet I couldn't even go into his room. A child in my first grade class had died of meningitis. Tuberculosis was also a killer.

To keep the rest of us from contracting George's fever, we were not allowed anywhere near his room. Mother boiled his sheets, towels and napkins, and almost everything to do with the food that she served him: dishes and silverware and drinking glasses. Trays were scoured with cleanser and bleach. These efforts at sanitation were not so unusual, as when we were babies, the diapers had always been boiled in the big boiler in the basement laundry. We were enjoined never to pick up anything off the floor and put it in our mouths. Mother insisted that we wash our hands before eating, when we came home from school, and almost any other time that we might have picked up any germs. This may seem excessive today, but it was the only defense available in the 1920s and '30s, when there were no antibiotics.

The new doctor showed up every morning with his black bag to see George. I waited in the hall in the hopes of hearing what he would say to Mother. After a few days he came out shaking his head and talking about an expected crisis. Then he left, and I saw that Mother had a worried look on her face. Would I lose my dear brother? I was terribly frightened.

Dad came home early from work that day; by then I knew that sick peoples' temperatures soared in the late afternoon, so I suppose that was why he had come home. He and Mother washed up carefully and went into George's room. Mother sat with George most of the time; we had a maid then who did the cooking and kept an eye on me and Linn. There was silence from George's room. I waited in my own bedroom across the hall, hoping to hear what would transpire. There was silence for a long time. My clock ticked from four to 4:15 to 4:30. Finally I heard Mother come out of George's room and say to my father, "You stay with him, I'm going to phone the doctor."

The only telephone in our house was the black Bakelite one on Mother's desk in the sunroom. It would be too obvious if I followed Mother down there to listen, so again I waited. Finally I heard Mother's footsteps coming back up the stairs and, this time, luckily, she didn't close George's door before she said to Dad, "It's okay, he says the sweating comes when the fever is broken, and we don't have to worry that much any more." I was so happy I danced a little jig in my room all by myself.

The boiling of everything continued, as did the quarantine. All that time Linn and I had not been permitted to leave the house because we might have carried the germs to other children. Now I was getting impatient for the quarantine to be lifted. It had been more than a week, and even though George was better, it would be several more days before the health department removed the quarantine signs.

Now Linn and I were getting bored and restless. Linn had his chemistry set in the basement which kept him busy quite a bit, and he liked to read. Of course, I wasn't allowed near the chemistry set, but I tagged along after the maid while she did laundry and cleaned house, and I even helped her with chores like polishing silver. There was no use asking Mother to read to me because she was still spending most of her time with George.

I remember the first day George got out of bed and walked out of his room; he was so weak that he had to hang on to the wall just to stand up, and he was all bent over, his brown, plaid bathrobe flapping around his ankles. It was hard to believe that my strong big brother was in such a weakened condition. However, he did recover quickly from then on and soon we were back in school, returned to our normal routine.

· · ·

As soon as I knew how to read, I loved books. Mother read to me quite often, and she helped me and George write letters to Donny in Chicago and to friends as well. From a very early age I could live in books, often learning more from a writer than I did from intimate friends. I would get lost in the life and problems of a fictional or real character, getting both education and escape from the same book.

We had a book of Bible stories with colored pictures that I liked very much. Those were my ancestors I was reading about. My favorite series was the twin books by Lucy Fitch Perkins. The main characters in each book were a set of twins, a boy and a girl. There were the Eskimo twins, who lived in an igloo; the Scotch twins who had a secret cave behind a waterfall; the cave twins of long ago; the French and German twins; and twins of many other nationalities. Perkins drew sketches on almost every page in black and white, and her storytelling and information were both well done and well researched. I wrote her a fan letter and still have her handwritten response.

I still remember poems from *A Child's Garden of Verses*. I can visualize the push-me/pull-you of Dr. Doolittle. I liked *Robinson Crusoe* and didn't care much for the boys' *Tom Swift*. It's hard to remember what books I read at what age, because once I began, I never ceased. I bless the novelists and writers, poets, historians and playwrights who have shown me so many worlds, so many souls, minds, hearts, have revealed themselves and humanity to me in their writing and made me want to write, too.

When I was eight, my family would go to Europe. Real-life adventure would replace books for a whole summer.

7

Europe

When I was eight years old, I had short black hair, round dark eyes and two front teeth that were too big for my face. I was still small for my age, and not at all athletic. But my parents were pleased with my progress in school, for I'd be starting fourth grade in the fall with children mostly a year older. Dad was willing to admit I was a good sport on expeditions and that I no longer whined or complained when I had trouble keeping up with the rest of the family. Mother alternately appreciated my push to be independent and scolded me for being "saucy," or impertinent.

The excitement that summer of 1929 was that we were going to Europe. When we set out for the Union Depot in downtown St. Paul, Dad wore a lightweight gray suit, a straw hat, and shiny black shoes. Mother had a dark blue linen traveling dress with a white collar, white gloves, a hat called a cloche in the same dark color as the dress, a white purse, and white oxfords. My brothers wore knickers and short-sleeved shirts and carried sweaters with argyle patterns. In the winter their corduroy knickers made a sound as they walked, but the summer ones were quiet. I wore my favorite dress—a white one with roses on it. Hat and gloves wouldn't be required of me until I was fourteen. I wore ankle socks and Mary Janes—black patent leather shoes with straps.

My parents had wanted to go to Europe for a long time, and their dream was about to come true. Their friends gave them a camera that took black and white movies, a first for anyone in their group, and they promised to bring back pictures to show everyone.

I had written *E-U-R-O-P-E* in chalk on the sidewalk and walked all around it. What did it mean? A place across the ocean, Mother had said. Different countries. Europe was lots of countries, I was told, but it was beyond my eight-year-old understanding.

Three months later I was happy to explain to all comers about Europe, England, France, and many other places. London was where the ducks ate out of my hand at St. James Park and where Piccadilly Circus was not a circus at all. Venice was where I fed the pigeons in San Marco Square. In Holland we went sailing on a boat with a red sail over water, the Zuider Zee, that would soon become land and grow crops. Most important, Frankfurt was where I met my German cousin, Marianne, and Kosiçe was where I met my Hungarian cousins, including a girl named Elephant Rosie.

Everything was new to me, starting with boarding the train in St. Paul. Soon after we settled in our green baize seats it was time to go to the dining car. The scary part was walking between the cars where they were hitched together and the noise of the wheels on the rails was very loud and everything shook up and down and someone had to hold the heavy doors open for me. When we got to the dining car, a nice Black man in a white coat told us about all the food we could have; there was a printed menu but he liked talking to us. The tablecloths were white and I had to squeeze in between my parents because the tables were really meant for four, but there were five of us.

Sometime after dinner another Black man in a different uniform, smiley and friendly, came and said he would make up our berths. I got to watch. He pulled out the seats, pulled down the upper berth and turned them into beds. It was like magic! Brushing my teeth in the train bathroom wasn't so great because there wasn't enough water to wash the toothpaste down the drain in the metal sink. Sitting on the toilet, I felt a cold breeze and when I looked into the bowl, I could see the tracks clicking by down there. I didn't like that at all.

The upper berth was fun, like the one at Bone Lake; I could peek out the green curtain to see if someone was walking by in the aisle. I could look out the window when we stopped, wondering where we were because train yards looked the same everywhere. When the train started again, Dad said it said "Good-bye Charlie, good-bye Charlie," but I just thought it said "Chooo-choo," long and short, over and over.

We got off in Quebec where people didn't even speak English. My mother had to talk in French. We stayed in a hotel that was like a big castle, the Chateau Frontenac. It was the first real castle I'd ever seen and I thought all kinds of fairy tales must have happened there. Many more castles and palaces were on the agenda. Mother told us children to keep diaries and checked in the evening to make sure we had done so.

I liked life aboard the Canadian ship. George and I enjoyed

the playroom for kids, but Linn was too old for it. He patronized the ship's library and walked the deck. We saw white icebergs looming toward us out of the deep blue ocean, and spouting whales. When it got rough, waves came up to our porthole, making it a beautiful green color and darkening the room. Mother and Linn were seasick, but Dad and George and I liked walking on the deck with the spray in our faces.

On June 27, we got up early and watched men haul automobiles and other cargo onto the docks at Liverpool. Once the rope broke. There was a mad scurrying around on the docks far below us, until a new cable was found. Luckily the boxes that dropped had hit no one.

Our English tour was standard—Oxford, Stratford, and London. When the chambermaid was working in our hotel room, speaking a cockney I couldn't understand, I told Mother she was too old and funny-looking to be a maid. Mother shushed me immediately, saying the maid could understand me even if I couldn't understand her, and that I must remember my manners and not be saucy.

On the continent, we traveled with a group of American tourists, the only family with children. Our courier, Curly, wore a special brown semimilitary cap so we could find him in a crowd. He saw to it that the steamer trunks, smaller trunks (later called footlockers), and other luggage were loaded on the ships or trains we took. My father had painted our luggage with yellow stripes for easy identification. We put our shoes outside the door of our hotel rooms at night and some unseen hands polished them. Curly kept us on our itinerary and delivered us to local guides in various art galleries, palaces and cathedrals. We kids liked him because he joked with us.

When we arrived in Frankfurt, after London and the Rhine cruise, we separated from the tour to visit for three days with Mother's cousin, Jessie, and her family. Jessie had grown up with Mother in Chicago and they had corresponded for many years. After her mother died, my mother was happiest when she could visit Jessie's household. The two girls were close friends, rode bikes together, and went to proper dance classes. When Jessie finished at Milwaukee Downer College, she and her mother made the grand tour of Europe, and Jessie met Emil Horkheimer, a wealthy and cultured German Jew. After a proper courtship, she married him and went to live in Frankfurt. He managed a textile business his great-grandfather had founded a century before, and was a relative of the philosopher Max Horkheimer. Jessie's family mirrored ours—she had two sons, Bernie and Walter, who were a few years older than my brothers, and a daughter my age, Marianne.

I stayed with the Horkheimers while the rest of the family stayed downtown in a hotel. Marianne had short black hair like me, but she was taller. Her manners were correct. She had an elderly nursemaid, Nana, who dressed her, walked her to school, even helped her bathe. As an American kid who had been living in the woods every summer weekend without running water or electricity and who had constantly struggled to be as independent as her brothers, I found this nothing short of babyish and ridiculous. As for Nana walking Marianne to school, I had no way of knowing that it was already dangerous for a Jewish child to walk to school alone.

Marianne's house was large and luxurious, although rather dark. I went to school and to sewing class with her. We couldn't talk much. Mother had coached me to say "Wie heissen Sie?"

(What is your name?), the formal address to an adult and, "Wie heisst du?," the familiar address to a child, a close friend, a dog or God. I couldn't believe the last and told mother it was nuts. I could ask Marianne her name, and she could tell me what I already knew. Still, we played with her toys. Her school—all girls—astonished me for two reasons. The children not only raised their hands to be called on but snapped their fingers. I thought that noisy and rude. To my surprise, at ten o'clock recess, every girl brought a little sandwich. When we got home at one o'clock, there was a big dinner served by a maid to the whole family. Unlike my father, Marianne's father came home for that meal, and went back to work later. At four there was tea. At seven there was supper.

I was also impressed by Marianne's handwriting class. My handwriting was pretty bad—I had not mastered the Palmer Method of penmanship with its ovals and pushups and admonitions to use the whole arm. Marianne painstakingly drew her letters on square graph paper. They were angular and perfect. Her sewing class consisted of a class in fine embroidery. I was astonished at the care and concentration she took, stitch after tiny stitch.

What I remember about Marianne's father, who was big, heavy, and distant, was one speech he made in English to my father at the dinner table. He said that anti-Semitism was so bad in Germany, and the economic situation so poor, that he felt his children would have no opportunities and must be prepared to go to live in America. Bernie immediately said he wasn't going to give up his opportunity to work with the great theatre director Max Reinhardt in Vienna, even if Germany was in trouble. Walter didn't want to leave, either. This was three years before Hitler became chancellor, but the Nazis were already a sinister enough presence for this farsighted man to grasp what his children must do. They didn't see it his way yet.

I picked my nose and when Mother scolded me and I was embarrassed, George said, "Well! you ought to be glad she can do it herself. I'll bet Marianne's nurse has to do that for her."

I learned later that although the apartment was large and beautiful and the family had many servants, almost everything they owned had been purchased before World War I. Emil Horkheimer was running the century-old textile business, but he was losing money.

We arrived in Paris on July 13 and met the tour group with Curly. Watching the Bastille Day parades and crowds from the hotel window was madly exciting; I learned about the French Revolution. I enjoyed the food in Paris and sailing toy boats in Luxembourg Gardens. But it began to rain and I noticed how dirty Paris was, so I was pleased when we went on to Avignon, where I loved the secret passageways in the Pope's palace. Mother taught me to sing "Sur le pont d'Avignon."

One of my father's problems on the trip was our ages. Ticket sellers for museums and events tried to charge him full fare for the boys, even though they were young enough to qualify for kids' rates. This was because Linn and George wore knickers or slacks, while European boys of the same age wore short-shorts; they didn't get long pants until they were sixteen. I was small for my age, so there was less of a problem. I was young enough not to require tickets. What made it even more difficult was that in mid-August, Linn, at thirteen years, had to shave for the first time. In Italy, where we traveled next, Father would present tickets, and quite often the gatekeeper would look at the four tickets and count in Italian up to five—*cinque*—pointing at me. Dad would try to indicate that I was too young—and for a while he gave me the nickname of "Chinky." It was a little more acceptable than a previous one: when I had complained at home that all the kids were blonde and I wanted to be a blonde too, Dad had informed me that if I went to Africa I'd be called a blonde and for a while he just called me "my African blonde." It didn't really help. Mostly I went by my real name, Ruth.

What I loved most in the Alps was walking into a cave in a glacier. The ice was a marvelous blue-green color and we carried canes with spikes in the bottom so we wouldn't slip on the ice. The people who climbed the Alps carried these canes, which were called "stocknagel," to which they would attach a metal souvenir of each mountain they had climbed.

Somewhere along the line, after visiting art galleries all over Europe, my brother George noted that Jesus looked Italian in Italy, with dark hair, and German in Germany, with blonde hair, and like the natives of whatever country we were in. I was impressed with that observation, my first lesson in cultural differences. In Holland George had wandered off from the guide and found the only "naughty" Flemish picture that we were not supposed to see. He was already rather a good artist and had a special way of seeing things; besides, he was creative at inventing games, and that made me get through the trip happily. I would always do what he told me, which probably helped him enjoy himself, too.

In Budapest, after leaving our tour group again, we stayed at the Gellert Hotel. We also swam in an outdoor swimming pool with waves like the ocean. That and the Gypsy music made a hit with our family. My father loved to play Brahms' Gypsy rhapsodies on his violin. The Gypsies didn't read music; they improvised, yet they followed their leader and stayed together.

We were excited about meeting my father's uncle, Lajos Guttman. He had a small, narrow shop where he sold watches. A man with a green visor and his sleeves held up with clips was working on some books in the back of the shop. My father complimented Lajos on having an employee, but Lajos said the man was from the government tax department and was going over his books to see how much he owed. My father lectured us that night about America and how Americans would never stand for that kind of government interference.

We went next to Kosiçe, then part of Czechoslovakia, traveling on another little European train on its narrow-gauge tracks. I remember meeting a group of people outdoors in a park, sitting at picnic benches. The oldest was my paternal grandfather's half brother, Solomon Feuerstein. My grandfather had translated his name to Firestone after he came to the United States. Jews in the Austrian Empire had been ordered to take German names at the end of the eighteenth century. Some officials sold them names, selling Goldstein (gold stone) for more than Silberstein (silver stone), while a name like Eisenstein (iron stone) was the cheapest. Feuerstein, which could also be translated "flint," was a place-name, and undoubtedly cheap as well. I thought that Uncle Solomon lived in a very poor place.

What amused me most was asking a little girl my age, "Wie heisst du?" Her answer sounded to me like "elephant Rosie," so I kept asking and she kept repeating, and we both giggled and giggled. I didn't know that some European children were taught to say their last names first—I think her family name was "Oliphant." When she giggled, I saw that some of her teeth were black and some were missing. She couldn't say the *th* in "Ruth" when I told her my name and that brought on more giggles. When I asked Mother about the black teeth, she had a chance to give me a great lecture about brushing my teeth and going to the dentist and how poor people couldn't afford to take care of their teeth.

My parents were communicating through Mother's German. They asked Uncle Solomon how old he was and he told them with a big smile that he was almost old enough for his bar mitzvah. He had a white beard and looked very old to me. My father explained afterwards that traditional Jews believed that the normal life span was seventy years, three score and ten according to the Bible, and to fool the angel of death they start counting over again when they reach seventy. So his uncle was almost eighty-three, since thirteen is the age of bar mitzvah. I took that in and couldn't quite fathom anybody being that old. My parents were in their forties, Donny was about sixty, and none of my other grandparents were alive.

When we visited the local synagogue, it seemed not only small but dingy to me. The impression of poverty was augmented because homeless Jewish men were permitted to sleep in the synagogues in Eastern Europe. It was hard for me to understand why the grand cathedrals were THEIRS and the dingy little synagogues were ours, in spite of a few exceptions like the beautiful synagogue in Florence and the large one in Budapest. At home we had a nice place to worship, but the churches were larger and grander. Abraham Heschel, a Jewish scholar of this century, wrote a moving piece in his book on the Sabbath. He said that Christians built their cathedrals in space and Jews built theirs in time—the continuation of the literature, the tradition, the religion—the real creation made by the Jewish people from Biblical times to the present is a three thousand-year structure in time.

On August 19, we went to Prague, where we could see the synagogue of Rabbi Loew, who made the golem. The guide took us to a tall building. It was almost one thousand years old, and we stepped down when we went in because in all those years the level of the street had become much higher than it was when the synagogue was built. It was called the Alt-Neu Shul (old-new synagogue). Inside it was dark, the walls were gray stone; the Gothic arches of the ceiling had a fifth rib to avoid creating a cross. The guide told us the body of the golem was in the attic—but it was only a pile of dried-up dust. I was very disappointed that we couldn't see it. When we were out on the street again I saw a clock with Hebrew letters for numbers; the hands turned "backwards"—counterclockwise—because Hebrew is read from right to left.

I shivered when we walked in the Jewish graveyard, where one stone was leaning on top of another, all so old—even Rabbi Loew's stone was there.

A surprise occurred when we walked across the bridge over the Moldau River. George and I trotted on ahead. In the middle of the bridge we stopped suddenly. There was a golden statue of the Crucifixion and above it many Hebrew words arranged in an arch, almost like a halo. It didn't seem right to us. Dad told us the Hebrew said, "Holy, holy, holy is the Lord," and that one of the medieval dukes had forced the Jews to erect this statue as a tribute to him so that he would "protect" them. In the middle ages, mobs of gentiles often attacked the Jewish ghettos, raped the women and robbed the people. Because of this statue, the Duke's soldiers presumably would keep the mobs away from the ghetto, where the Jews were walled in to live in crowded slum conditions.

From Prague we went to Carlsbad, then to Berlin and finally to Bremen, where we boarded another Canadian ship and headed for Montreal. Out in the Atlantic, my poor mother became seasick again. I played in the playroom with George and the other kids on board, and we formed the Knights of the Square Table. On September 5th we saw a sparrow and then sighted land.

At the end of the diary I wrote, "I had a wonderful time. Thank you." I concluded with one of my unoriginal poems:

> "The wind doth wirl,
> And the water doth swirl,
> for the ship in her course doth go
> the masts are high
> and the sailors nigh
> For the ship in her course doth go."

For an eight-year-old girl who had spent all her life in Minnesota and Wisconsin, the European trip was a stretcher of mind and spirit. I was amazed by the size and beauty of the ocean and the mountains. I learned how one country differs from another in language, history, and geography. When the sun came through the stained glass windows in the cathedrals, I enjoyed the colors splashed on the stone floors. On the outside I looked for the amusing gargoyles, which I liked better than the classic Greek sculpture in the museums. I absorbed many images of art and architecture, even if I didn't understand the concepts.

I experienced my Jewishness in new ways. We had warm welcoming family in different places. My Hungarian great uncle, poor but pious, educated in Jewish texts but not in Western learning, was typical of many Eastern European Jews. My assimilated German family with their Western university educations and European manners typified the Jews of Western Europe. I saw that whether clinging to the old traditions or embracing Western ways, Jewish life in Europe was uncomfortable, although in 1929 it was not yet threatening. I knew we were lucky to live in America.

8

Five Gold Coins

Once, when my parents were out for the evening, I peeked into the top drawer of my mother's mahogany dresser. I knew she kept her treasures there—her string of real pearls, which she had worn that evening, and a blue enamel brooch with little diamond chips. When I opened the drawer and got on my tiptoes to peer in, I was surprised to see a pile of gold coins. I took them out, saw that they had a queen on one side and foreign words on the other side. I couldn't imagine what they were doing there, and I couldn't ask because of course I shouldn't have been looking in the drawer in the first place. I hurriedly put them back and went to my room. Now I knew a mysterious secret, and I wondered how I would ever get an explanation, but a few weeks later I did, in another surreptitious action.

Mother and Dad were having a party, probably to celebrate one of their friend's birthdays. With no formal organization, the little group of close friends—about six couples—entertained each other often with dinner and cards and always celebrated birthdays together. Our maid, Ann, would be joined by the cateress, Mamie Green, a thin black woman of whom I stood in awe. Mamie was not only a wonderful cook, but she also told Ann what to do and most amazing of all, she could even order my mother around. Her food was marvelous and we kids were always fed a wonderful dinner in the kitchen before the company came. Then we were supposed to go upstairs to our rooms and stay there.

My father not only had a delightful verbal sense of humor but he was also a great practical joker. He had noticed that excelsior—the shredded bits of wood used for packing in those days—looked like chow mein noodles. That was the famous night when he asked Mamie to take some excelsior he had found, put it on plates and cover it with a sauce that made it look like chow mein and then serve it for a first course. We three kids sat on the stairs, out of sight of the party but able to hear what went on. Everyone seemed cheery, Dad was telling one of his jokes and they were all laughing. In those days, people really dressed up for parties, and even though I knew there were just twelve people at our dining room table—its absolute capacity—the women wore long dresses and the men tuxes or dark suits. It made things festive. Before television and in the infancy of radio, adults had to be good at amusing themselves, and my parents and their friends always seemed to have a great time. They knew each other well—all belonged to Mt. Zion and many of them were childhood friends of my father's. Some of them played the piano; some sang; some told stories; and they had a great time playing cards, the women choosing bridge and the men pinochle.

We knew when the fake chow mein was served because

there was a sudden quiet. I wished I could see their faces when they bit on the wood.

Suddenly a male voice called out, "Milt, you joker, what the hell is this stuff?"

We could hear my dad and mother laughing. Dad said, "Ansel already swallowed some. It won't hurt him."

All kinds of voices joined in the chorus of asking what it was. They finally got their answer and joined the laughter. Now we knew Ann would serve Mamie's real dinner. There would be homemade consommé, roast stuffed chicken, and a picture-perfect platter of vegetables, red beets in the middle, then green peas around it, and parsley for decoration. Ann would pass Mamie's home-baked rolls, butter, salad in molds, and always relishes: Mother's homemade dill pickles, pears poached and colored red and green, watermelon pickles, celery sticks stuffed with cheese. No liquor then because of Prohibition, but it didn't seem to stop them from having a great time. Maybe Mamie's super-rich chocolate cake for dessert was giving them a sugar rush.

While they were eating, I wandered out of my bedroom and took my hidden place on the stairs. Mother must have been seated at the card table nearest the stairway because I could hear her clearly. I didn't recognize the other voices. They were talking about when their parents or grandparents had come to the United States, a subject that was unusual at that time. People wanted to be all-American and not to remember their immigrant origins. Suddenly I heard Mother say quite clearly that her father had been born in Rio de Janeiro. The rest of the group exclaimed in considerable surprise.

"His parents were from Alsace," she said, "and my grandfather owned a diamond mine in Brazil. They didn't stay long because my grandmother got some tropical fever after my father was born. They ended up in upstate New York. My father was quite small when they came to this country."

She was asked if she had any diamonds from the mine and laughed and said, no, all she had was a handful of gold coins.

I bided my time. One Sunday afternoon, my father announced he had made a special arrangement with a friend: he was going to take the boys to the railroad roundhouse and they would get a ride in a big steam engine. Of course I asked to come, too, and was refused. Only room for two, and not for little girls. I began to cry. My mother took me in her arms and we lay on the couch and she cuddled me and stroked my hair. "Don't feel bad," she said. "Should I tell you a story?"

The men were out the door. "Yes," I whispered, "tell me about your grandma and grandpa."

She said, "My mother's parents were from Berlin. They were solid German burghers, and came to Chicago with some money, so they immediately went into business. My mother was eight years old when they came."

"Why did they go to Chicago?" I asked.

"Because that was the frontier when they came—it was as far west as the railroad went right after our Civil War."

I was wily. "What about your other grandparents?" I asked.

She told me it was a long story and it has remained one that still puzzles and interests me. Jacob Cain and Fannie Benjamin, newly married in their home country of Alsace, then part of France, went to Rio de Janeiro in the 1850s. The trip must have been long and rough because most transoceanic trips at that time were by sailing ships; steam was in its infancy.

They problably had to travel from Alsace to Marseilles, perhaps by rail, and then by ship through the Mediterranean to Brazil. They may have stopped at Bahia, the bulge of Brazil that extends furthest east toward Africa, and then worked their way down the coast to the glorious huge harbor of Rio.

Brazil was an independent kingdom then, its king a descendant of the King of Portugal, the colonial power until Napoleonic times. The only railway in the country went from Rio to this king's summer palace, which was a small copy of the Pink Palace in Lisbon. Roads were poor. Transport in a few places was by stage coach and by horseback where the roads were inadequate. Freight was pulled by oxen at their slow pace of about five miles a day. Almost all laborers in Brazil were slaves. The majority of the population in the 1850s when the Cains arrived was black. My mother felt ashamed to tell me that her grandfather had owned slaves. I think this is why she had never mentioned this amazing story before. She wasn't sure if Jacob had owned the diamond mine or if he worked it for someone else. Jews were often in the diamond business, then as well as now. This began because although Jews were barred from traditional craft guilds, diamond cutting was a new trade in the late Middle Ages, so they could enter it. They probably continued in the diamond trade because diamonds are so portable and can be hidden easily when a person is in danger. The same situation created many Jewish violinists in eastern Europe in the nineteenth and early twentieth centuries; a violin was far more portable than a piano or a cello. A person could run with diamonds or with a violin.

At any rate, Jacob Cain was operating a diamond mine, and the mines were in mountainous country a long way from

Rio. He already spoke French and German, but he had to learn Portuguese, ride to the mines on his horse, supervise the mining, the shaking down of sand and ore until the diamonds were found, and the shipment back to Rio for cutting. Guards had to be hired to prevent the slaves from stealing diamonds; other guards had to go with the loaded oxcarts and the men with diamonds in their saddlebags because the backcountry was full of bandits.

Meanwhile, Fannie Cain waited in Rio. The houses there were three stories high, painted pastel colors—pink, blue, yellow—as in Portugal, and built very close together on streets leading to the central square. Facing the square was the cathedral, and across from it the long low government buildings. On the other two sides were a few shops, and houses with shops on their first floors. The public well was in the center of the square. Slaves carried water from the well to the houses; they carried human waste and garbage to the ocean and dumped it in. Human transport was used almost as much as horses or mules. All the work of loading and unloading ships and carrying the goods into and out of the city was done by slaves, who were often crippled by the heavy loads they carried. It was a cruel society and it must have been hard for Fannie, coming from Alsace, to live there. She, too, had to learn the language and find women friends to keep her from being lonely when Jacob was off at the mines. The Jewish population was very small because the Inquisition had operated in the New World well into the nineteenth century.

After a year or so, Fannie became pregnant. When Maurice, a fine baby boy, was born, she became ill. (Maurice was my mother's father.) Jacob tried to find a good doctor, of which there were very few, and the doctor could only tell him that she had some kind of a tropical fever. They probably used cold packs to reduce the fever, but she remained quite weak. Letters went back and forth to Europe by slow boats, and soon the Cains decided to go back to Europe for Fannie's health. I don't know what happened to the diamond mine. There was another long boat ride. This time, adventurous Jacob found a job in Berlin. Fannie recovered and soon their daughter Bertha was born. But Jacob was restless. The United States beckoned as the land of opportunity. Jacob and Fannie, who must have been very adventurous herself, may have sailed to Boston or New York. At any rate, they ended up in a little town called Whitehall, New York, where Jacob kept a general store and learned English.

Long after I heard this story I went to Whitehall and discovered it had large derelict buildings on what had once been a main street. I couldn't find Jacob's store, but I did find out why he had chosen the place. Whitehall is located near ship locks on the canal that connects to the waterways of Montreal and New York City, and also connects to the Erie Canal. Jacob's knowledge of French certainly was a help to him there. After they arrived, their third and last child, Eli, was born. Their three children were born on three different continents in days when travel was far from easy. They were daring people, risk-takers. Today only people sailing ships for pleasure go through the locks at Whitehall, but until the railroads were built, and even after, canal traffic carried many of the commercial loads in this country. My grandfather Maurice grew up, finished high school in America, spoke French, German, and English, and headed west to Milwaukee, Wisconsin. My mother said

"Maurice Cain" was a French version of "Moses Cohen" (or Moses of the priestly family), which made my grandfather a special person. I thought having five gold coins almost a century old from my great-grandparents' sojourn in South America made my family mysterious and romantic.

9

Spring and Summer

Passover, which comes every Spring, is every Jewish child's favorite holiday. Each year we celebrated with my aunt and uncle, Rose and Allan Firestone, and their two children, Phyllis and Dick. There was a tragedy in their lives: their first son, Danny, who was my age, had died when he was four years old during an emergency appendectomy. Afterwards, Dick was born. Phyllis was three years younger than I, a beautiful little girl with golden curls. Of course I was envious of her looks. Dick was almost six years younger than I, so he didn't appear on the scene until I was in school, and I had no interest in babies. My Aunt Rose was a pretty woman, taller and younger than Mother, who envied her appearance.

One year we put on our best clothes and went to Rose and Allan's for Passover. Allan played the piano, singing us a little love song he had written about Rose. We never called it composing. Allan was a sweet man, smiley and pudgy. I never saw him lose his temper. My wiry, heavily dramatic father, eight years older than Allan, played the older brother, advising and "helping" frequently.

The table was set beautifully, with flowers and all the Passover goodies—the sweet haroses, the boiled eggs, the greens, the special plate with matzos and the shankbone of a lamb, the horseradish known as bitter herbs. We used the gray Reform haggadah, with pictures that I loved to look at. Dad and Allan took turns reciting from the book or extemporizing. There were always times of laughter and of seriousness. It was fun for everyone. Our book omitted the ten plagues, so that the story wouldn't present anything nasty. According to midrash (Jewish legend), the angels and the children of Israel rejoiced after the crossing of the sea, but a voice from heaven told them to stop because hadn't God's children (the Egyptians) been drowned in their chariots?

The Seder, or Passover dinner, teaches with food: eggs represent springtime, haroses, made of chopped apples with sugar and nuts and other good things (the recipe varies according to different families), represents the mortar with which the ancient Jews cemented blocks to build buildings for the Pharoah. Bitter herbs make us taste the bitterness of slavery. The lamb bone reminds us of the last plague (the Reformers couldn't leave that one out) when the children of Israel fled from Egypt after the death of the firstborn Egyptians. Traditionally, Moses is never mentioned, lest he be worshipped instead of the One God. But Father talked about him as a great leader and thinker.

I enjoyed the Passover food but always worried that Rose would serve peas and carrots—the peas were canned—because I couldn't convince Mother that peas and carrots made me nauseous. She might make me eat them, and then I'd have to run to the bathroom to vomit. Luckily, after I was six or seven, food didn't nauseate me anymore. At Passover, asparagus was favored as a spring vegetable just arriving on the market, so I might be spared.

Passover is the great festival of freedom; maybe for me at that time it meant the promise of freedom some day from parents. It celebrates the exchange of slavery for the long wandering in the wilderness, and the coming home to the promised land: "We were slaves in Egypt and the Lord led us out with a mighty hand." In those days before the Holocaust, it was possible to feel that Egyptian slavery was the worst thing that had ever happened to us, that somehow, some way, regardless of persecutions and pogroms elsewhere, we would survive, with the help of God. We were thankful to live in a blessed land.

The best part of the Seder for children comes after the meal, providing we weren't too sleepy from staying up late and tasting the sweet red kosher wine. First, after dessert, which was always sponge cake with the first strawberries of the season, the children were set loose to find the hidden matzo—the afikomen—without which the Seder could not continue. Somehow we never saw the adult who hid the matzo. For once we could throw the sofa pillows around, look everywhere, move anything, because the Passover couldn't finish without that special piece, which had been broken and had to fit with the piece Dad or Allan had kept. By now the adults were all laughing.

The child who found the afikomen always got a prize. Once I got a whole box of wrapped hard Passover candies with fruit fillings made in Vienna. I was told how they had been shipped over the ocean in a big boat.

Mother and Aunt Rose had to buy matzos and ceremonial

wine from the temple. Grocery stores stocked no Passover supplies in those days, and everything else—after the major house cleaning—had to be baked or cooked at home without any leavening. Baking cakes that rise only with egg whites takes a special talent.

After the afikomen was found and redeemed and the child who found it was given a prize, the service could continue. A child went to open the door for Elijah to join our dinner. A little later we looked carefully at the silver wine cup that had been filled for him, and Dad and Allan convinced us that the wine had gone down. Elijah had been with us and had taken a sip. Then Dad and Allan, with their beautiful bass and baritone voices, sang the wonderful children's ditty about the only kid "my father bought for two zuzim," and we all chimed in with the chorus in Hebrew. It seems that the cat ate the kid, the dog bit the cat, the stick beat the dog, the fire burnt the stick, the water quenched the fire, the ox drank the water, the shochet (kosher slaughterer) slaughtered the ox, the Angel of Death took the shochet, and the Holy One, blessed be He, slaughtered the Angel of Death. Each time, each item is repeated to the chorus of "an only kid." I liked the pictures and loved the song. Only as an adult did I learn some of the allegorical interpretations—the kid is Israel, subject to persecutions from those cats from Assyria, dogged Babylonia, cudgel-wielding Persia, Rome, the Saracens and the Crusaders, etc.

This song was written in the thirteenth century in Europe, expressing faith in final redemption by God. Maybe it also said: Take note, tyrants of our own time. Or maybe it was a promise of victory over the inner enemies that eat away at our souls. Some day, these enemies, like death, will ultimately be overcome by the Holy One.*

And there was more fun: "Who knows One?" Someone asked, and everyone answered as quickly as possible, "One is the God of the world!" and so on through two tables of the covenant, three patriarchs, four mothers in Israel, all the way to thirteen attributes of God, as taught by Maimonides. Everyone laughing and out of breath when the final thirteen were recited backwards.

We sang "God of Might" (Adir Hu) and "America the Beautiful" before it was all over. Later, we celebrated and augmented those Seders of our childhood, in the odd places my husband and I found to live in during World War II when he was in the army, in the home we built in Minneapolis and with our four children. Who can ever finish thinking about slavery, freedom, and exile? About escaping from the prejudices and habits with which we enslave ourselves? About building community that will balance the freedom we found in the empty wilderness of the Sinai desert or in the anonymity of American cities? And yes, to build freedom in community takes at least forty years, whether we speak of our own lives or of Jews in all the places where we live.

Not long after Passover, we'd finish school for the year and start summer vacation. From the time I was nine years old I went to camp for two weeks in the summer. The first time was at a Camp Fire Girls' camp, although I was not a Camp Fire Girl. For the next two or three summers, I went to Girl Scout camp. These camps were fun for me, although I went without knowing any of the other girls. I liked nature study, being out-

* These explanations are from Rabbi Richard N. Levy, ed. and trans., *On Wings of Freedom, the Hillel Haggadah.*

doors, swimming, and the usual songs and high jinks. I was with girls my own age, unlike my friends in school, most of whom were older. The athletic activities weren't competitive, so I could enjoy them without losing or being the last one chosen for a team.

One time at Girl Scout camp, we all became excited about going on an overnight hike. We made our sleeping bags out of blankets, since the kind now available probably didn't exist, or anyway not in the price range of Girl Scouts. We made lists of all the supplies we needed, including the inevitable graham crackers, chocolate bars and marshmallows for the evening campfire. We carried heavy army-surplus canvas pup tents. We were taken partway in the camp jitney and left in a wooded area. From there we carried all our equipment in big knapsacks until we found a pleasant place where we set up our tents with considerable difficulty. It's not easy for ten-year-old girls to pound stakes into the hard ground with the back of a small hatchet.

We built our campfire, had our supper and sat around singing songs. It was a moonless night and the stars were very bright. Our counselors started telling ghost stories around the fire. As the flames died down and we looked into the coals and heard their voices coming from bodies mostly unseen in the dark, things got scarier and scarier. "Where is my golden arm?" was repeated in a ghoulish voice as part of one of the stories. Finally it was time to go to bed, and with only the light of our dim flashlights, we crawled into our pup tents—two in each one. There was one tent for the two counselors and five tents for us ten girls. It was hard to go to sleep with the ghost stories vibrating in our spines. My friend and I whispered for a while until a voice from the counselor's tent demanded quiet. I managed to pick out a few rocks from under myself and discovered that the tree roots could not be moved. Somehow I curled around them and went to sleep.

Suddenly there were loud noises outside our tent, noises made by big animals tearing through the brush. We could hear leaves crunching under foot and branches being pushed aside and thought immediately of tigers and elephants. But we were in Minnesota, where we didn't expect anything bigger than squirrels or rabbits or a shy deer. The ground was shaking. What if these creatures stepped on our tents? We didn't know whether to get up or to lie still. The noise continued. We were terrified when we heard a scream from the next tent. "Something's pulling on our tent!"

Where were our counselors? I turned on my flashlight. My friend cried, "Don't! We better not turn on our lights, they might come and get us." So I turned the flashlight off.

Suddenly something pulled at the flap of our tent—an animal? It was our counselor and she was laughing. "It's only a herd of cows," she said, "and we're making them go away."

I had been on plenty of overnights, usually the climax of any camp experience, but this is the one I remember best.

Calderwood, Mr. Calder's resort across Bone Lake from our cabin, was not doing well during the Depression. My father bought the small, white horse Mr. Calder had kept for his guests to ride. Her name was Snowball. Father paid $25 for Snowball including her saddle and her bridle. Snowball now lived on the Anderson's farm, near our cabin, with our neighbor's horses and cattle. Theoretically, we could ride her whenever we went to Bone Lake. Snowball was very docile when I or other children rode her. For older kids and adults, she could gallop at a pretty good pace. I would dig in my heels and get her to trot or occasionally canter, and now and then I would fall off. I was pretty skillful at it and never got hurt. Snowball would stop after I fell off and look at me with a really disgusted expression on her face. I would get up, take her bridle, and lead her home, unless I could find a fallen log or something else to step on in order to remount.

Later I took and enjoyed riding lessons and horseback riding. Horses never frightened me. Snowball, however, developed a different personality whenever she'd been out in the pasture for a week or two. She wasn't interested in being caught for riding and she was very clever at avoiding capture. Unlike the cows, she was not intimidated by the shepherd dogs. It was my brothers' job to get her out of the pasture on each Friday when we arrived at the lake. Sometimes my father went along and got a good laugh at her tactics. She would stand quietly, watching the boys, but just as they thought they could get the bridle on her, she'd toss her head, wheel away and take off. If worse came to worst, we would wait for evening when she habitually came in with the cows, expecting a few oats from Mr. Anderson.

Since people were not patronizing Mr. Calder's resort, one summer he rented it to a group who used it for a Catholic girls' camp. The camp was called Wabigoniss, which is reputed to be an Indian word meaning "little flower." (Saint Theresa of Lisieux was called the little flower.) My parents decided that it would be very convenient for me to stay at Wabigoniss during the week when they were in town, so long as I could come and spend the weekend with them at the cabin. The women who were running the camp agreed to this. My father said it was good for a child to learn about different people and religions. I had a good time at that camp and was one of the younger campers, so I believe they spoiled me a bit. One counselor told me my hair was so beautifully black that it had blue lights in it.

The activities were very similar to those at Girl Scout camp: nature study, swimming, arts and crafts, and hiking. By now I was good at identifying trees, wildflowers and birds, and was allowed to lead a hike occasionally. What was different, of course, was the grace before meals, which I said, but I didn't cross myself. The other thing which intrigued me greatly was the girls' behavior prior to the weekly arrival of a young priest. They began to whisper and giggle and go off into corners with each other, sometimes blushing, other times screeching with surprise at what was being said. I found out that all this excitement was in preparation for confession. It seemed to me that they were thinking up sins so they could spend time talking privately to this young, handsome priest, even though it was explained to me that he couldn't see their faces and that they only heard his voice. A small room in the main building had been set up as a chapel, so when they received their penitence, such as three rosaries, five "Our Fathers," or seven "Hail Marys," they would go to the chapel and kneel to say the proper prayers.

Afterwards, things quieted down and I could see that the girls seemed happily contented. I decided that confession was really a great idea, and I wished it was part of my own religion. Of course, I didn't go to confession and the staff, knowing that I wasn't Catholic, didn't expect it of me. They had mass on Sunday, but I was across the lake at that point. I had gone to mass with my neighborhood friends at St. Mark's, anyway. The church was not as beautiful as the ones I had seen in Europe, and the ceremony intrigued me and repelled me at the same time. The music, the priests in their special dress and the choreography all attracted me. But the idea of wine turning to blood made my stomach queasy.

I knew that Judaism had Yom Kippur, the Day of Atonement, when we fasted and asked for forgiveness for the things we'd done wrong in the course of the year. I had taken part when the whole congregation stood up and recited a long list of sins, some of which I couldn't identify. Mt. Zion was small enough so that children could attend services with adults. I knew there were also daily and weekly prayers for repentance in the synagogue's ritual. The individual character of the Catholic practice at camp appealed to me more than the collective confession, even though I realized that most of these girls had not done anything that I considered sinful in a major way.

One fall day after my first summer of camping, Mother took Dad to work so she could have the car; she then picked us up at our various schools and took us to the eye doctor in the Medical Arts Building downtown. I was taken along because there was no one to care for me at home. I was often a tag along. The boys both had glasses, but I didn't. I sat there and watched the doctor check their eyes with the big E and the other letters on the eye chart. My brothers were both near-sighted, but they weren't allowed to wear their glasses when they had gym or roughhoused with other boys. Both had argued with my father about it, but he said glasses were too expensive and that was final.

The doctor looked at me and said to Mother that maybe he should test me, too. I sat on the little round stool and read the first couple of lines. Pretty soon there was a very heavy frame on my nose and I was saying, "That's better" or looking at a bunch of blurs. The doctor told my mother I certainly needed my eyes "corrected." Linn needed a new prescription, too, but George was okay for now. Down we went to Meyrowitz's shop on the main floor. Mother knew the man who put different empty frames on my face and she chose the one he said was strong but cheap. It looked pretty strange to me, but I wasn't consulted. My glasses would have round, fake tortoise-shell rims. I liked the gold-looking frames better.

A few days later I went downtown on the streetcar to meet Mother and get my glasses. They felt heavy on my nose. I kept seeing the edge of the frames. The floor had moved farther away from my feet when I stepped. I wanted to tear them off, but Mother said I'd get used to them, and we set off for home. On the way she reminded me she'd been cross-eyed as a little girl. They had operated on her eyes, but didn't know much about it then, and the result was that one of her eyes turned out. She said I was lucky that I was only nearsighted and astigmatic. Poor Mom; poor me.

But as we were walking home from the streetcar, something miraculous happened. I looked up at a tree. Of course I knew trees had leaves, but all I had ever seen up there was a green blob. Suddenly I could see leaves and branches! I even saw a bird!! It was marvelous. I started skipping, an activity I had flunked in kindergarten, but now was good at. "Yay, yay, I can see the leaves," I chanted and Mother laughed and took my hand and walked faster to keep up. She even apologized for not having noticed that I was nearsighted.

That night Father lectured me on always taking care of my glasses and not wearing them in gym. Now I was happy—I had a good excuse for never being able to catch a ball. A few days later when Donny arrived for a visit I heard her and Mother whispering that it was a pity I had to wear glasses, because my big brown eyes were my best feature.

"Do they ruin my beauty?" I asked. Mother assured me that when I got older and went to parties I wouldn't have to wear them. It wasn't much reassurance; I knew I was too short, but now I realized I must be homely, too. Still, it was wonderful seeing the leaves on the trees and reading the signs when I was riding in the car. I enjoyed taking my glasses off, looking at all the blurry things, and then putting them back on and seeing outlines get miraculously clear and sharp.

"Donny"
(Meddy H. Cain, 1867-1932),
Irma's stepmother

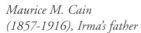
Maurice M. Cain
(1857-1916), Irma's father

Marriage photo (August, 1882).
Rosalie Goodman (1860-1926)
to Jacob Firestone (1850-1928),
Milton Firestone's parents

Milton Firestone (1886-1952) in St. Paul law office, 1919.

Irma Firestone
(1886-1957), ca. 1945

Firestone home (1919-1950), 1866 Portland Avenue, St. Paul

*Milton P. Firestone,
ca. 1950*

Cabin at Bone Lake, Wisconsin, 1930

Linn (age 13), Ruth (8) & George (10)

Ruth Firestone, ca. 1926 (age 5)

Ruth and George Firestone on photographer's donkey, 1925

George, Ruth &
Linn at Bone Lake
1925

Mount Zion Temple Confirmation Class, 1935
(Ruth Firestone, First row, second from right)

Ruth Firestone Brin,
Wedding Day
(August 6, 1941,
age 20)

Vassar College, Convocation, September 22, 1940

Howard Brin,
Wedding Day
(August 6, 1941,
age 21)

Ruth & Howard Brin,
Aberdeen Proving Ground, 1943

Ruth Brin & Judith,
December 23, 1945

Ruth & Deborah, December 1954

Howard & Ruth Brin, with Aaron, Judith & David
(2861 Burnham Boulevard, Minneapolis, 1951)

1960s Jewish magazines (includes poetry and essays by Ruth F. Brin)

10

Starting U High

My brother George drew a cartoon of Mother pushing me in a baby buggy to the door of U High. It made me angry and it made me laugh in spite of myself. I started seventh grade in January of 1932 at the age of ten. Almost all my classmates were a year or two older than I; all were taller. I was confused, not only by having to find my way from one classroom to another but to different buildings for lunch (Shevlin Hall), chorus (Pattee Hall) and gym (Norris). I had to carry a purse with a fountain pen. In grade school, we had steel pens with an ink well in each desk. At U High, with its one-armed desks in every room, we had to carry pens; a fountain pen in those days cost about $5, the price of a good pair of shoes or a cotton dress. I was always losing my purse or my pen; once when I couldn't find the purse after a young people's concert in Northrop Auditorium, I rushed back to my seat. It was gone. I missed the bus home and had to call Mother, tears streaming down my face as I reported two offenses—losing the expensive pen and missing the bus. Dad was so exasperated that night that he wouldn't talk to me at all, and I cried again.

Another problem was finding someone to sit with during lunch. All the girls who had started U High in the fall had their own little cliques; yet, when I sought out those who had come with me from Alpha Class, they had found new friends or had been assigned to a different lunch hour. I wouldn't cry about this, but I sat down alone and some other girl, whom I immediately assumed was as out of real social life as I was, joined me. It was a few weeks before each of us managed to find a group to eat with.

Why U High? (The University of Minnesota Lab school was part of the College of Education.) The Depression had deepened in Minnesota somewhat later than on the East Coast. St. Paul voters had refused bond issues for the schools; there was talk of not paying teachers, or of paying them with scrip, a kind of government IOU that merchants might or might not honor. Classes were large—forty or more children in a room in elementary school—and large classes in junior and senior high as well. Students in public high schools had to pay for transportation, carry or buy lunches and buy books, as we did at U High. The only additional expense for it was the tuition of $25 a quarter, or $75 a year; my father could still manage that. The rub was that children had to have a "high IQ" to be admitted.

And why was I only ten years old? At that time, children were promoted or failed or skipped every semester. After I learned to read in grade 1-B, I skipped 1-A and went to 2-B. Our classes were so large that children of equal learning ability, even if they were of different ages, were put together.

For 5-A, 6-B and 6-A—the last three semesters of elementary school before junior high, I was sent to Alpha Class. It was another way of skipping, for we did three semesters' work in two. We met with a blonde young teacher named Miss Converse, brought our bag lunches, and had a good time. Neither boys nor girls were afraid to show that they knew answers to questions. There was a camaraderie that I enjoyed. In Alpha Class we didn't have gym; I loved that. I started U High in January, joining the seventh graders who had begun in September, because of the machinations of the mother of one of the other girls in my Alpha Class whose son was a senior. The U High class that fall had several more boys than girls, so they accepted four girls from our Alpha Class.

Meanwhile, at home my mother decided it was time for more sex lectures. She had begun these earlier but now she made sure I knew all about menstruation, childbirth, how the mother was impregnated, and birth control.

Mother told me how Margaret Sanger, a nurse, had been horrified by the death of a married woman with several children. This woman had lived in the slums; she and her husband couldn't make enough money to feed the children they already had. When the woman found herself pregnant, she tried to abort the fetus and she bled to death. Sanger found out about birth control by traveling to England and France, where it was legal, but when she came home, the federal government put her in prison for giving poor women birth control information. Mother told me how lucky I was to be born in a time when women could plan their families and when "every child could be a wanted child" as I was, she assured me.

I had begun to show embarrassing signs of maturing, like budding breasts. I began to make sure that my brothers didn't see me partially undressed, something I'd never bothered about before.

George was only a year ahead of me at U High, while Linn was a senior. George had finished sixth grade (Alpha Class) in February and started seventh in public school, then had to start again at U High in the fall because it was on the annual system. I had gained a year and he had lost a year. Mother had wanted to send him to St. Paul Academy after he finished Alpha Class. SPA was the preparatory school where "rich boys" went; girls went to Summit School. But when Mother went to the headmaster at SPA with George's grades, he didn't look at them. He just said that he already had one Jewish boy in that class so he couldn't take another. Our dinner table discussion about this was a mixture of anger and resignation; my parents weren't surprised at the rejection.

They knew that the "best" colleges restricted Jewish enrollment; that made it easier for prep schools like St. Paul Academy to deny admission to Jews. At U High, whose faculty included many Ph.D. candidates, I recall only one Jewish faculty member during my six years there. Few colleges and universities would hire Jews; many would not admit us to their graduate programs. Public universities technically did not have policies of discrimination, but individual department heads could be discouraging, especially if the job market realistically offered no place for a Jew.

My own medical problems weren't over. There had been a lull in my troubles with Mother about food. When I was about nine years old I'd finally begun to eat enough to suit her, but now, as I started junior high, she realized that I was overweight and began telling me to cut down on carbohydrates and sweets. When she noticed that I was tired all the time, (she called me a "tired old horse") she took a good look at my neck and decided

I had the goiter common in our region. This time I got to go to Dr. Rosenthal, trained in Vienna, which mattered to my parents. He was a much sweeter man than my former pediatrician, which mattered to me. Of course Mother was right. At that time I was convinced that she was always right, which was very discouraging. I got iodine in my orange juice every morning.

I had read a haunting short story about a beautiful woman who was thyroid deficient. When the man who had power over her got angry, he would withhold her thyroid supplement. She would gain weight, get puffy, sleepy, and stupid, become a sort of zombie with dry skin and hair, hardly able to get out of bed. Then if she promised to please him, he'd put her back on her thyroid and she'd become thin, vital, and bright again. Would it be like that for me? I was frightened.

Riding home on the junior high bus, I would sit in the backseat with two other girls and whisper about menstruation on some days and how to be popular with boys on other days. Mother hadn't mentioned that some girls got cramps; she insisted later that she had never had any cramps and so assumed I wouldn't either. I may have known all about the physiology but the older girls introduced me to terms like "the curse" and "falling off the roof" and how terrible the cramps were and the fear that boys could tell if you had "the curse." None of us had "started" yet. We were waiting for this mystery to be revealed. We read the Kotex pamphlet, *"Marjorie May's Twelfth Birthday"* but still had questions.

One morning when I was eleven, I found blood on my toilet paper. I had a belt and a sanitary pad already supplied, of course, so I put them on. Weird—some strange bulky thing between my legs. As we waited for the bus that morning, I told my brother George. He didn't say anything, but turned away and looked down the street. Now, even our private moments of intimacy were gone. That was when the gate of my childhood really clanged shut. Living in the same house on the same street with the same family, I was in a cold new world. I had lost my best playmate, George, and had no one else anything like him. I was eleven years old, four feet, eleven inches tall, and overweight. I was struggling to understand Donny's terminal illness, still dreaming that I would grow slim and beautiful, with blonde curls, but I knew I was short, dark and dumpy. The only good thing was that now I had an excuse to stay out of gym once a month. Even if I didn't have cramps, I could follow the example of my elders and go lie down on the couch in the office of the girls' adviser and get a pink slip to stay out of math class. Those were the immediate rewards of maturity!

I thought that with my brother George going to the same school with me everyday our old closeness would continue. I was disappointed to discover that George, at thirteen, had moved into another world, a world of adolescent boys who didn't want anything to do with kid sisters, and probably with any other girls or women. When his U High or scouting friends came to visit I was expected to leave.

George became an Eagle Scout and an enthusiastic camper and canoeist. He liked science and did well at school in spite of his poor spelling, which enlightened teachers didn't seem as annoyed about as Mother was. He wrote rather well. His cartooning and drawing were original and funny, and he was popular for his sense of humor.

But I was deeply hurt and lonely now that I could no longer be his playmate. Even at Bone Lake, he often brought along another boy and I was left standing on the shore while they took off in the new canoe.

To add to my troubles that year, Donny came from Chicago to live with us because she was sick again, as she had been when I was a baby. As before, the piano was moved into the living room and a bed was put in the sunroom, which was no longer our playroom. Maybe we were too old for a playroom—we each had our own bedroom, after all. If the boys teased me and I screamed or cried, Mother came down hard on me: "You're upsetting your grandmother. You're old enough to know better!"

Dr. Nippert came every few days and tapped Donny's legs, which meant inserting a needle to remove the accumulated fluid. Her heart wasn't able to pump it up. I watched once but not again. My dear Donny, who had taught me to do needlepoint, who had made beautiful paper costumes for me, who had sat up so straight at the table and demanded good manners of us, was gone. The old woman whose pale face looked so sad, whose white hair was all scraggly around her on the pillow, seemed like someone else. There was even an unpleasant odor sometimes. I tried to stay away.

I thought about how when Dad yelled at the boys in one of his temper tantrums, Donny would announce, "The great man at home!" and defuse the situation. We could all laugh. Dad was mercurial—he could joke and have us all laughing, yell and have us all scared, cry and have us all crying. Even Mother couldn't stop him as effectively as Donny could.

One day in school I got a message that Dora, one of Mother's friends, whom I knew well, would pick me up after school. She arrived with that I-know-something-you-don't-know look that children learn to recognize in adults. She said that Mother had asked her to take me to buy overshoes. We went to the store and got a pair of black rubber overshoes with buckles, which went over the uncomfortable Oxfords with Cuban heels that I now had to wear to school everyday. The dress expected of girls included tan wrinkly lisle stockings held up by a garter belt, skirts, often a blue serge skirt with a middy blouse, or a plaid wool dress with white cotton collar and cuffs that could be taken off for laundering. Boys had to wear slacks, jackets and ties.

On the way home I learned Dora's secret. She told me Donny had died that morning. I knew I was supposed to cry, and I pretended. But I felt nothing at first, then hollow, empty, numb; something died inside myself. It was my first real experience of death.

That death festered in me for many years. I went to the funeral and the rabbi talked about the soul being immortal. Afterwards Mother said that the important thing was keeping people alive in our memory because that way they still influenced us and our lives for good. I didn't ask Dad, because basically I never dared ask him about his beliefs and he never volunteered to discuss them with us children. It upset me that I couldn't believe in the immortality of the soul.

To relieve myself I wrote a poem, the first time I recall turning to writing as a way out of an emotional crisis.

II

Entering My Teens

One of my jobs at Bone Lake in the summer was helping Mother make the beds. The boys would be outdoors after breakfast, often helping Dad with some project. We'd make quick work of dishes, sweeping up, and making up the cots on the screened porch. The summer I was twelve, I pulled apart one bed to see a big yellow stain. One of George's friends had slept there. The bed smelled bad.

"Did this kid wet his bed?" I asked my mother in astonishment.

"No," she told me, "he had an ejaculation and probably a wet dream."

I asked her what a wet dream was, and then I wished she hadn't told me. Why did I have to know that boys dreamed about girls and then their semen spilled out on the bed? I had longed to be popular. Now I wished that I didn't have to look at another boy. Was he thinking about putting his penis in me? George's friends, it was true, hardly looked at me at all. I was a nuisance of a kid sister to them. I had wished one of them would think I was pretty, even though I was convinced I was homely. Now that I heard Mother's explanation, told to me like a science lecture, calmly and objectively, I didn't say a word to her. Inside, I wished sex would go away.

But it wouldn't. Now when I looked at boys and men, I wondered if they were having erections. I didn't want to think about it, but there it was. In the fall at school another girl and I would whisper and giggle about our bachelor math teacher. Did he get excited when that gorgeous practice teacher showed up? Someone had heard that he was "taking out" the new young art teacher… would they get married? When the seniors got drunk at beer parties, did they "do it?" Oh no, we told each other, maybe some necking, but not going "all the way," not until after college… or were we too innocent? Sometimes I shared the information Mother had given me because even without experience, I wasn't as ignorant as some of my friends. But what was the point of knowing all this stuff if nothing ever happened?

Externally I was a good girl going about my piano lessons, religious school, U High, camp and the lake in the summer… and I was learning. But not music. The piano was back in the playroom. I was busy all afternoon with school work, sometimes with extracurricular activity and Girl Scouts, so I had to practice after supper. Dad would be lying on the couch in the living room under his newspaper while I pounded at the piano. Suddenly a bass voice would erupt, "B-flat; don't you know you're in the key of F?" I would cringe. He had absolute pitch. He played the violin so well when he was twelve that he had played a solo with the St. Paul Symphony. He could have been a professional musician, but he had chosen law as a more secure way of life. When I finally got to some simple Bach and

Mozart, mangling them, he admitted I'd never make it. I was through with music lessons—what a relief! Shortly after, I dropped Scouts as well.

I now had religious school on both Saturday and Sunday because I was in pre-confirmation class. Our teacher, Mrs. Zack, taught home economics in the St. Paul public schools and directed Sophie Wirth Camp in the summer. She was small and birdlike, with a sharp little face and a firm manner. Students in her classes sat still and listened. She taught us Jewish history: Biblical, Roman period, Medieval European, the emancipation after the French revolution, American. She taught us how the prophets stood for social justice, which many of our families tried to practice. She taught us about Jewish customs, like keeping kosher, which probably none of our families practiced.

One of the results of my years with Mrs. Zack was that I became a star pupil in my tenth grade Ancient and Medieval History class at U High. I already had a kind of timeline in my head. Besides, I loved my teacher, Miss Bovee, a young woman who wore her dark hair in a braid around her head. She was working on her doctorate in history, but she often smiled at me, a quirky, slightly twisted little smile that I found very attractive.

When we got to the Crusades, I went to see her in her office during study period.

I challenged her, "Our textbook makes the Crusades sound so noble," I said, "but you know when they marched through the Rhineland, they considered the Jews to be infidels. So why wait till they got to the Holy Land? They killed them, robbed them, raped the women, and totally wrecked many communities."

She asked me what my sources were and I could tell her. "Besides," I explained, "that's when the rabbis made a rule that the child of a Jewish mother is a Jew. So many women were raped that they wanted to accept the children, not shame the mothers who had had such a miserable time."

"Good for you," she told me. "I know something about religious persecution because my ancestors were Huguenots in France and the Catholics did their share of murder and rape to get rid of them. I don't think that's in most high school text-books, either, but I always talk about it when we get to the Reformation." She patted me on the shoulder, and suddenly I thought she was the most wonderful person in the world. "Keep on questioning," she told me, "that's how you learn and get wise!"

I loved her; I wrote her poems I never sent; I went to talk with her in her office when I could think of something impor-tant to talk about. I wanted to grow my hair and wear it in a braid around my head like hers. Mother said, "It's your hair, but I can tell you long hair is a nuisance. I felt really free when I bobbed my hair." I kept it short. A year later my "crush" on Miss Bovee evaporated.

More than ever, I wanted to be a writer. My English teach-ers always liked my work. The first time I had something pub-lished in the *Campus Breeze*, U High's biweekly newspaper, I came rushing home with the paper in my hand to show it to Mother. I felt totally depressed when she wasn't home and the maid said, as she so often did, "Your mother will be home at five o'clock." I knew Mother was out helping her German refu-gees, but how about me?

When I was thirteen, my Uncle Allan, who was then in the advertising business, came to my rescue and submitted one of my poems to the only local magazine published in the Twin Cities at that time. *The Golfer and Sportsman* printed my poem.

It felt wonderful to see the poem and my name in print. My parents were proud of me and I basked in their praise. Here's the poem:

STORM

Gray day,
somber, desolate, dreary,
Gray day
Then with a mad leap
Rain
It dashes down the sky
stumbles on green earth
and wakens her to
Rhythm of thunder
   rumbling, howling
   mumbling, growling
Rhythm of rain
   running, prancing
   leaping, dancing
Rhythm of wind
   shrieking, moaning
   howling, groaning
Rhythm of lightning
   flashing white
   clashing bright
And then the storm
Grows tired of play,
Goes to sleep,
and leaves
Green day
bright, cheerful, lively
Green day.

Once I passed my fourteenth birthday I learned to drive. The car was a square, black Dodge, a few years old. The new cars were becoming streamlined, but when I was fourteen in 1936, we certainly couldn't afford a new car. The whole family was trying to teach me to drive, since there was no such thing as driver's training. As a new driver, I had to learn how to use the choke to start the engine, pulling it out as I stepped on the gas in neutral gear, and pushing it back before the car got too rich a mixture of gas and flooded. I had to learn to use the clutch with my left foot, shift gears with my right hand, and use my right foot appropriately on the gas and brake pedals. I had to arrange cushions to sit on so I could see out the windshield.

My first instructor was my father. At first he was patient, but with him patience was an effort. It took coordination to drive a car in those days, and I frequently killed the motor or stripped the gears, making a sound that made me cringe. Fortunately, after I had learned the basics, Mother took over. I would drive around the quiet neighborhoods where there wasn't much traffic.

Forty-five miles per hour was considered fast, and it was, on the narrow paved roads and the many gravel roads. Every time we left to go to the lake, if Dad was not coming with us because of business, he would say, "Don't forget the keys to the cabin and don't drive over forty-five miles per hour." It got to be so frequent a saying that we all joined in the chorus. Another of Dad's remarks that we could all join in with was spoken whenever he drove under a bridge and we were the passengers. He would say, "Duck, or you'll be a goose." I didn't figure out the pun for quite a while, since he said it from the time I was about two years old.

At first, the road to Bone Lake was paved until we got to Taylors Falls. Beyond that, the roads were gravel. When Linn was learning to drive, I had frequently hit my head on the ceiling of the car when he went over big bumps on the gravel roads. Of course I cried and created a fuss, but somehow he didn't learn to slow down. I thought that was malicious on his part, but my parents tended to be angry at me—not him.

I particularly recall one Sunday afternoon in the spring when we drove out of St. Paul and Dad decided I should try driving faster on a paved country road. He pulled over on the shoulder near Tanner's Lake, which was then in the country but is now a suburb of St. Paul. Dad was in the front seat with me; and Mother, George and Linn were in the back. I began driving smoothly, to my satisfaction, and continued down the road. Dad said I could go faster, and I did; but then a farm wagon appeared in front of me. I took my foot off the gas, shifted into a lower gear and put my foot on the brake. I had shifted down at too high a speed, causing the gears to screech. Suddenly Mother and Dad were both telling me what to do and the boys were guffawing. I heard the cacophony. Instead of passing the wagon, I pulled back to the shoulder, parked, and said, "I'll only go out with one teacher, not four." It was not the first time I had been defiant; still, I felt proud of myself for defying my entire family at once.

I learned to drive finally and sent 25 cents and a return postcard to the Minnesota Transportation Department to get my driver's license, which arrived on my fifteenth birthday. There was no examination of any kind, and farm children were allowed to drive cars and tractors when they were twelve. Being able to drive didn't give me a great deal of freedom because we had only one car, and I was low man on the totem pole as far as using it went.

The following summer we went to Bone Lake and I complained to my mother because I was missing one of the very few parties I had been invited to all year. It was a Saturday morning, and my parents were expecting an older couple to visit and stay overnight. My mother's answer was a shock. She said, "You know how to drive. The Levys are coming this afternoon and we can get a ride back to town with them, so take the car and drive yourself home. Go ahead and go to your party!" I was really afraid but I didn't dare say so. Mother gave me the car keys and key to the house in St. Paul and said, "Drive safely."

I collected an apple from the ice box, piled my cushions on the seat, and got in the car. Everything went well until I came to a railroad crossing. A steam locomotive had passed by and started a fire in the weeds and grass on both sides of the tracks. That was common in those days, because sparks from the coal-fired engines could fly out the smoke stack. This fire was sending up billows of smoke; I couldn't see whether anything was coming down the track, or if anything was on the other side of the tracks. I knew that the narrow gravel road curved after crossing the railway. If there were a car on the other side, and I couldn't see it, I might hit it. I stopped and sat there in a state of paralysis. If I went back to the lake, I would be defeating myself in front of my mother. Of course I realized that she was always pushing me out of the nest, but as I sat there, I became angry with her. Didn't she know I was just a little girl? How could she have exposed me to so much danger? What to do? I sat some more. Finally I remembered that, after all, trains always blew their whistles when they came to crossings. What concerned me was that this crossing was so small that there were no bars or anything to stop traffic when a train was coming, just one of those "RR Crossing" signs. I didn't hear anything. I wished that the wind would blow the smoke away, but it didn't. Finally I gulped and with tears in my eyes shifted into first and drove through the smoke across the tracks. There was no other car in sight. The rest of my trip was uneventful, but long. I was tired when I got home, but I know I bathed and dressed and went to that party. I can't remember a thing about it. I finished the day with a great sense of accomplishment, even though I was still miffed with my mother for making me drive seventy-five miles home alone.

12

Confirmation

Mount Zion Temple was on the corner of Avon and Holly streets, a brick building with a school on one side that held a few offices. The main sanctuary had a small dome and an impressive entrance up several steps to some white columns. At least it was impressive when I was a child, although the building, like the congregation, was small. Perhaps two hundred families were members in the 1920s. I got a ride there on Sunday because Dad was either president of the Temple, chairman of the Sunday School, or had some other major job, so he was there, too. When confirmation class came along, there were extra classes after regular school, so I went on the streetcar.

Mt. Zion, at that time, was classical Reform. That means the service was mostly in English with a little Hebrew; the prayer book was the *Union Prayer Book*, which omitted certain prayers that were not acceptable to the rabbis who edited it. For example, the prayer for rain, which repeats the idea from Deuteronomy that God will give rain to the just and the good, and withhold it from the wicked, was omitted as not being consistent with modern thought. Men and women sat together, men did not wear yarmulkes (skull caps), and the rabbi was the sole occupant of the bimah, or platform in front of the ark, where the Torah scrolls were kept. He wore neither robes nor a prayer shawl, but appeared in what was then called a morning suit. There was a choir loft with an organ played by an excellent organist. The choir sang more than the congregation, but we all knew some hymns very well.

At that time Reform had substituted confirmation for bar mitzvah. The children were kept in the educational system until they were in the tenth grade, fifteen or sixteen years of age, instead of thirteen. Also, boys and girls were treated alike. I don't think anyone in St. Paul had heard of a bat mitzvah for girls, although the first one had already been held in New York City. The bar mitzvah is for a boy at the age of thirteen to signal his maturity as a Jew and to show his learning by being called to the Torah and reciting the required blessings.

Both boys and girls were to be confirmed as a class, after completing our studies of the history, customs and beliefs of our people. Confirmation takes place in the spring at Shevuot, which is a thanksgiving for the spring harvest—the first fruits— as well as a commemoration of the giving of the law, that is, the ten commandments, at Mt. Sinai.

Growing up in Reform, I never felt discriminated against as a woman. Families, men, women and older children, sat together and joined in prayer and song, while in most Orthodox synagogues women still sat in a balcony behind a curtain and were neither seen nor heard during services. In Reform Judaism as I knew it, women were involved in all aspects of temple life.

By the time I was fourteen, learning about Jewish beliefs in confirmation class, I was beginning to question just about everything. I didn't know whether there was a God or not. Ever since Donny's death, I could not believe in immortality of the soul. When I asked questions in class the rabbi either gave me routine answers that I had heard before or brushed me off—and this was the one year we had him for a teacher. Early that spring he had a heart attack and had to stop working for some months. Our confirmation was put off until the following fall, at the end of Succot, the fall harvest festival that also celebrates the end and beginning of the annual cycle of reading the Torah. In Reform congregations in those days, the readings were short selections from the larger portion assigned to each week.

In our Bible studies we had learned the Genesis stories in the early grades; read Psalms later; and, as we got older, concentrated on Prophets, because Reform emphasized the demand for justice and righteousness—ethical behavior—as one of the two essential elements of Judaism. Monotheism was the other. I liked the ideas of the prophets, but not the idea of a punishing and rewarding God. I didn't see it in my life or in the lives around me. By then the Depression had fallen like the rain, on virtuous and wicked alike.

My brothers had been confirmed. The services were held in the evening and afterward, there was a reception in the homes of each youngster. With ten or twelve in a class, and with no one living very far from anyone else, it wasn't too hard to make the rounds in one evening. Mt. Zion was a small and close community. Mother got pretty involved in having a properly lovely reception. We didn't have a punch bowl and a friend offered one to Mother, saying she didn't like it and never used it anyway. When the punch bowl somehow was broken, Mother of course offered to have it replaced, expecting her friend to say something like "Never mind." Instead, her friend's husband became quite angry, because apparently the punch bowl had come from his mother. My parents replaced it. Punch bowls didn't like our house. For George's reception, she borrowed again, and another one was broken again. Dad said he'd get a stainless steel bowl for the punch at my party, and I didn't know whether or not to believe him. But since my confirmation was in the fall when it was chilly, the solution was to serve tea and coffee and forget the punch. Mother's beautiful Bavarian china with the gold edges and the brilliantly colored flowers would come out, and the embroidered linens, and the sterling flatware.

When the rabbi met with us again in September, he was thinner, but seemed well. He announced that we each had to write a speech of two to three minutes, and if we didn't feel able to do that he would help us. He assigned subjects based on our Biblical and historical studies. In the spring the sanctuary would have had flowers, but now it seemed we would have not only chrysanthemums but also some autumn leaves. I was supposed to carry them up as the whole class marched in together. I would put the flowers in a vase and give my speech about Judaism and "the beauty of holiness."

I was a stubborn girl and had no intention of letting the rabbi write my speech. We had gone to the lake the weekend after Yom Kippur and hiked through the woods where the leaves were turning yellow, red, orange and copper. The soil was moist and black under foot and smelled of the woods. We stopped to look for the ghostly Indian pipe, but it had not reappeared, although fungi often do grow in the same place, year after year. In the pasture we spread out, filling our baskets with the brown mushrooms growing at the base of old oak trees. Dad hiked to the fence to cut bittersweet. It was a misty day and began to sprinkle a little. I was cold and I felt like crying. The good days of spring and summer were over; work and winter lay ahead. I'd be stripping the leaves off the bittersweet and hanging it up to dry to brighten a little of the coming dreariness.

And so, when I wrote my speech for confirmation, I wrote that adolescence was the autumn of life, and maturity was the winter. This exactly mirrored my feelings of loneliness and depression. Childhood had been my spring and summer and it was over. The rabbi demanded to see our speeches and called me into his office, smoking his smelly cigar, to tell me that youth is the springtime of life. He took out two poems by famous poets and read them to me to prove it. We came to a stand off and he referred me to my father. My father tried to put on his judicial tone, but I could see he was amused by the whole thing. That made me angry and I ran upstairs to my room and wouldn't talk to him. Ultimately he and the rabbi toned down my talk but let me keep my idea and I practiced my two-minute speech and liked the cadences of it. No one ever said anything to me about it afterwards; very possibly no one listened to those speeches anyway.

But I had an even more difficult problem with the rabbi. Judaism insists on monotheism, but over the centuries other matters of belief have varied in one way and another. The central core is Torah and Talmud, but there is loads of room for interpretation. My rabbi decided that it would be a good idea for us to recite a credo on the bimah. This he took from

Maimonides, a Medieval Jewish philosopher whose ideas have never been totally accepted as final truth but are considered the important work of a brilliant man.

Maimonides' creed had thirteen points about God, who is one, eternal, the creator (I wasn't sure what was meant by God and if I believed in God at all). Maimonides said the Torah was true and unchangeable. (But hadn't Reform changed a lot of the rules?) He taught that the soul is immortal and is rewarded or punished in the world to come. That last part galled me the most: for some reason, since Donny's death, I still couldn't believe in immortality.

I was supposed to stand in front of the congregation with my classmates and recite all thirteen points as my own beliefs. I couldn't do it. I couldn't believe in a world to come where the good were rewarded and the evil punished. That seemed too much like the Catholic ideas of heaven and hell that my friends had explained to me. Certainly in this world reward and punishment didn't match up with the recipients. One of the boys in my class had actually stolen our last test out of the rabbi's study and read the questions out loud to all of us. I was shocked and upset by him. I was going to be more honest than he was. I was angry and unwilling to lie in public, to claim I believed something I didn't believe or was doubtful about.

I didn't tell my father about the boy who had cheated; everyone passed the test anyway. But I did tell him in no uncertain terms that I refused to be confirmed. There was no point in talking to Mother, who was easier to talk to; the temple was Dad's department. Dad tried to calm me down but I wouldn't be quiet. I showed him the credo we were supposed to read aloud and stood there defiantly. He said it would be a disgrace for the family if I weren't confirmed. He said my brothers had done it and I would be sorry later if I didn't. He said he was an officer of the temple and people would be critical if I refused. None of these arguments convinced me.

Finally he asked me to do something for him, to do him a favor. That was a new experience. I didn't know I had the power to do anything for my father, much less a favor.

"You go through with it," he said, "you stand up there but you don't have to say anything. Just stand there. That way you're not lying and I'm not in hot water."

That was what I did.

I went through with confirmation, and I even went to postconfirmation class because the subject was comparative religion and visiting different churches interested me. But what confirmation had confirmed for the most part was my serious doubts about being Jewish.

13

The Deepening Depression

My parents had two good friends named Delight and Fred Rosencranz. I called them Aunt Dee and Uncle Fred, which was the way we children were taught to address our parents' close friends. Otherwise, of course, we always called our friends' parents *Mr.* and *Mrs.*, and seldom called any adults by their first names.

Uncle Fred was a construction engineer working for the Great Northern Railroad. Aunt Dee was always attractive to me; she was small, curly-haired, with a puckish face. She had been a singer in light opera productions before she married. She played the piano and occasionally gave singing lessons. They were one of the few non-Jewish couples with whom my parents were on a very informal basis. I remember going to their house and having them visit us.

One night at dinner Dad wore a very troubled look on his face. It seemed in those days that all important conversations took place at dinner. We were sitting at the new light-finished mahogany dining room set that my parents had bought before the Depression from Yungbauer and Company. Dad sat at the head of the table with his back to the mirror on the sideboard. Mother sat at his left because she didn't like to look at herself in the mirror. She also told me, "When you get married, don't sit across from your husband—sit next to him; he might get tired of looking at you eating." Linn sat at the foot of the table and George and I sat on Dad's right. There was something sacred about our own places when we were children; we always insisted on having the same chair at dinner.

The evening, probably in early 1932, when Dad came home with bad news about the Rosencranzes remains in my mind. He wore his most tragic expression, his deep voice trembling, his mouth drawn down. He said that not only had Fred lost his job, but the railroad was firing many people—hundreds would have no jobs.

My mother said feebly, "I wonder what they can do?"

Dad replied, "Fred told me they'd paid off the mortgage on their house, but that he has very little savings."

Linn piped up, "Well, at least they'll have a house to live in."

Dad answered, "Not unless they can pay their property taxes."

Mother said, "Maybe Delight can give more music lessons."

A few months later, Dad came home again looking tragic. I was beginning to expect some of these tragic announcements, because they seemed to be coming rather frequently. My father was chairman of the Ramsey County Welfare Board. The board was responsible for relief and financing Ancker Hospital, the county hospital. Dad was appalled by the poverty they had to deal with; he didn't like the idea of federal interference, but

recognized the need. Many of the volunteer social work agencies that mother was associated with were running out of funds,
even though they had more people than ever to take care of.
Some of the township and county relief funds were close to
exhausted.

Meanwhile, I no longer took dancing lessons with Miss
Rothfuss, but was signed up for elocution lessons, and enjoyed
learning how to "recite." Mother was president of Central Community House, located near the capitol in an old rundown
neighborhood that was "slum-cleared" years later. The head
resident was Miss Biederman, who came to our house for dinner quite often. When Mother took me to a performance of a
musical or pageant in which children my age acted and sang I
wished that I could participate in something like that. There
was no community center or park recreational program in our
neighborhood, and our public school was too busy teaching
the three R's, too budget constrained to put on plays. Most of
the families in Miss Biederman's neighborhood were Jewish,
many relatively recent immigrants; other Jewish families were
served by West Side Neighborhood House, directed by Miss
Currie, who also showed up at our dinner table, as did Miss
Grodinsky from Jewish Family Service. I half listened to those
conversations, knowing many of the kids went to Sophie Wirth
Camp, which I had visited with my parents. The kids seemed
to be having a wonderful time and I loved swinging on the
swing hung from a big oak tree while Mother consulted with
the director and the cooks. I always thought it would be fun to
go to Sophie Wirth; later, when I was sixteen I became a counselor there.

Although my father did not vote for Roosevelt, my mother

did. We all listened to his hopeful fireside chats on the radio and his programs did seem to offer some new solutions to our economic problems. For example, Fred Rosencranz soon had a job with Works Progress Administration (WPA). He was developing some plans for building bridges and trails in some of the city parks. The problem was that like many professional people at that time, he was extremely embarrassed and ashamed to have to take what he called government welfare. Interestingly enough, my brother Linn was taking singing lessons from Aunt Dee; he had a bass voice which had some of the resonance of my father's.

Another topic among my father's frequent tragic reports was the rise of anti-Semitism, both in St. Paul and in the country at large. There were cells of Silver Shirts, a Nazi-style group, in the Twin Cities and small Minnesota towns. Luke Rader and Rev. Riley were a couple of anti-Semitic Christian ministers in Minneapolis whose diatribes were broadcast on local radio. On national radio, we couldn't bear to listen to Father Coughlin's hateful messages out of Detroit. Dad felt that he had lost some of his Gentile clients because of anti-Semitism.

What affected me most occured one evening when Mother and Donny, who both understood German very well, were listening to a speech by Adolf Hitler on the radio. It must have been in 1931. This was the first broadcast of his speeches, and the two women had talked about listening to it for days. I heard an angry man ranting and raving. They were looking at each other with absolute horror: open mouths and wide-open eyes, their heads shaking in disbelief. The speech was short. Afterwards they talked to each other in German and I asked them to speak English. They were so excited and upset that they hadn't even realized they were speaking the language they had been listening to. They told me Hitler was talking about murdering the Jews.

"But of course," Donny said, "the German people are well-educated and cultured. Surely they will not listen to this man!"

"I'm not so sure," Mother said. "When we were in Germany, Emil was already talking about how serious anti-Semitism was in the country."

My grandmother began to talk about the people of Goethe and Beethoven and how she still couldn't believe the Germans would listen to this maniac. But Mother said, "What about Wagner?" Donny shook her head. I knew they didn't like to listen to Wagner's operas, but I didn't know why. They explained that Wagner had believed the German people and their legends were superior to all other people. He had been an anti-Semite.

George chose to go to Harvard College and then to medical school at the University of Minnesota. He would have to do very well at Harvard, because the medical school, like most in the country at that time, had a Jewish quota; my understanding was that it would not admit more than ten percent Jewish students, even if their records were better than others.

One evening a young cousin, Don Frankel, came to dinner. Don had just started at the University and announced that he was going to major in aeronautical engineering. My father put down his fork. "But you won't be able to get a job," he said. "The big corporations don't hire Jews."

Don smoothed back his black hair and grinned a kind of artificial smile at Dad. "But it's bound to be a big field in the future," he said, "and I'm fascinated with flight."

"You'll be wasting your time," Dad said, "and your mother's

money." (Don's father had died a few years before.) My father looked serious. "It might even be difficult to get into graduate school," he added, explaining about Jewish quotas and how few Jews ever got to be professors.

In Don's case, he and my father were both right. Don couldn't get a job when he graduated around 1939, but a few years later when the war industry began, he did find work in his chosen field. Even after the war, a friend of mine who had a doctorate in chemistry explained to me that big corporations opened their research departments to Jews, but for many years they were not put in line for any kind of management positions. That finally changed, probably in the 1970s.

Although the University of Minnesota admitted a limited number of Jews to the medical school, my brother George did well at Harvard and was admitted. Minneapolis hospitals did not allow any Jewish doctors on staff; patients had to be admitted through other doctors, a situation that wasn't remedied until Mt. Sinai Hospital was built by the Jewish community well after World War II. My brother, after military service and all his training, didn't stay in Minnesota to practice.

Dad felt that his sons would be most successful as independent professionals like himself. A few Jews could make it if they had enough capital to start a business, and there were many Jews in small retail operations. During the Depression, large chain stores were beginning to replace the small Jewish grocery and candy stores known as Mom and Pop operations. So Linn studied chemistry at the University; I used to play with the models of atoms and molecules that he brought home which were something like Tinker Toys, only different colors. After he graduated in 1936 with a Phi Beta Kappa, Linn went off to Harvard Law School where he became an editor of the *Harvard Law Review.*

Growing anti-Semitism and poverty were not the only difficult parts of the Depression. In the mid-1930s the drought and the dust storms began. I can remember summers when, no matter how often a housekeeper dusted, the top of everything was covered with very fine silt. The wind never stopped blowing. Temperatures rose to over one hundred degrees, and the only air-conditioning was in a few movie theaters. Often when we sat down to eat we would find grit between our teeth, because of dust on our lips and on the food. It was quite impossible to sleep in the ovens of our bedrooms. We began by taking our pillows to the front porch, but even that, with its roof and screens, held the heat. After a few days it seemed as if everybody on our block was bringing an old blanket or sheet, laying it out on the dried, spiky lawn, and sleeping outdoors at night. The winds died down in the darkness, but the ground was so dry that little coolness rose from it.

Sometimes during those hot summers we would take our sandwiches to Lake Nokomis and swim and picnic for supper. The water was low in the lake and lukewarm, but it still felt very good. Occasionally our parents would take us to an air-conditioned movie or even for a ride in the car to "cool off." We were lucky that we could continue to visit Bone Lake because it really was cooler out there; if it was one hundred degrees in town, it might be ninety degrees at the lake.

One day in town, George tried the great experiment touted by the newspapers of frying an egg on the sidewalk. It worked. Mother was angry because he had wasted food and, of course, you couldn't eat an egg fried on the dirty sidewalk. Dad laughed.

In May 1934, a truck drivers' strike began in Minneapolis. My social studies teacher at U High told us how the workers were being exploited—they were paid $12 a week and were not allowed to have a closed shop or to organize. The employers, who had formed a group called the Citizens' Alliance, were the powerful people in the city. My teacher was pleased when the Farmer-Labor governor, Floyd B. Olson, negotiated an agreement between the Union and the employers. My teacher believed that capitalism was failing and that some form of socialism was going to be necessary, as in Sweden or even in Russia. If not, fascism would develop.

In July, in the dust bowl heat, the strike broke out again because employers had not permitted the Union to continue organizing. All deliveries in the city were again stopped except for those to hospitals, and now farmers were allowed to set up informal markets. A violent episode occurred in the Minneapolis market area (Sixth Street and Third Avenue North) between the police, who were trying to break the strike by moving a truck covered with fully armed officers, and the strikers. Sixty-seven people were wounded and two killed. That night, after Mother had sent me out to buy the "extra" newspaper a boy was hawking in the street, we read the account with gasps of horror. Nothing like that was supposed to happen in our civilized community.

Father came home bitter and sad. He said the election of Olson had encouraged the lawlessness of strikers who didn't care if people had ice to preserve their food or enough to eat, for grocery shelves all over the Twin Cities were empty. Allowing the farmers to set up markets on the street this time, he predicted, was a poor solution. Some crops would rot in the fields and the milk would be dumped on the ground even though there were hungry people in town.

"But Dad—." I was glad George was willing to speak up because I was amazed at my father. I had been so naive, expecting that well-informed adults like my father and my social studies teacher would agree. George mentioned that the strikers didn't have a living wage and had agreed to terms in May. But Dad said that both sides had failed to abide by the agreement. Floyd Olson had imposed an ambiguous set of terms. Dad claimed the strikers were led by people from out of state, Communists who were followers of Trotsky, who were extreme. It was true that the Dunn brothers, two of the leaders of the strike, were considered Trotskyites, but they had lived and worked in Minneapolis for several years. They had also been expelled from the Communist Party.

George then advanced the argument that capitalism was failing and we would have to become socialist. This really annoyed my father. "I believe in this country," he proclaimed. "I believe in our form of representative government and in our economic system. Don't you let anyone fool you—socialism is as bad as fascism. Sooner or later it becomes dictatorship."

Mussolini, Hitler and Stalin were firmly in power in 1934, but the violence of their regimes had not been fully reported. The Japanese had invaded China (Manchukuo), but the United States was most deeply involved that summer in strikes in many of its major cities.

Mother thought the police had behaved in an inexcusable manner by shooting at unarmed civilians. Dad was willing to admit that they had been extreme because he wouldn't disagree with Mom in front of the kids. The discussion ended without ending. I wished I could go ask my social studies teacher some more questions, but school was out. In August the strike was finally settled when Governor Olson sent in the National Guard to support the strikers and to quiet the city. The workers got the right to organize and establish closed shops, but they received no wage increases.

Some days that summer at the lake while George was busy with his friends, I hung around with Mrs. Evans, a grandmotherly woman who had a cabin not far from ours. Mr. Evans had owned a hardware store in a small town, but my parents explained that he had lost it because of the Depression.

Sometimes when I went over to visit, Mrs. Evans was working in a steamy kitchen, canning fish her husband had caught. She also put up the vegetables he grew, except for the potatoes and rutabagas, which he put in a root cellar. She told me that Mr. Evans could cut all the wood he needed to keep them warm in the winter from Mr. Anderson's pasture, so long as he shared some of the wood with the farmer. He traded some hours of work for apples and chickens from another farmer. Swapping work for goods, or just one thing for another, was a common way to get by without cash in those years.

One day I saw Mrs. Evans wring a chicken's neck, wait till the headless thing stopped running, then toss it into a pot of boiling water and start pulling the feathers. I started to run away and she laughed. She said she'd grown up on a farm and slaughtering chickens had been all in the day's work. She invited me to pick raspberries with her the next day and I went along, enjoying plopping the berries into her tin pail. She would make jam that evening after they had some fresh berries for their supper. She told me in fall she'd can applesauce and make apple butter. She baked her own bread. I saw that living off the land was hard physical work. I was too young to wonder how they would survive old age and limited physical capacity.

What brought the plight of the farmer home to me was a visit Dad and I made to Mr. Cook's farm, which was about a mile from our cabin. We had gone to buy fresh vegetables because Mr. Cook was a very good truck farmer. Mother and Dad had numerous farms earmarked for buying different products: one for eggs, one for chickens already cleaned, another for flowers, especially gladiolas. Mr. Cook supplied us with tomatoes, green beans, lettuce and squash.

When we got there, he said, "I don't know what to do. I can only get 10 cents a bushel for my green beans. They are all ripe now and if I wanted to harvest them I would have to hire help. For 10 cents a bushel, I can't hire anybody and I can't even pay for the gas to drive my truck into town to market the beans." I remember Mr. Cook as a tall thin man with black hair and piercing black eyes. He threw up his hands, and at that moment, I really felt sorry for him. He said, "Go ahead and pick all you want; I won't charge you anything." He turned around and went back into the unpainted house where he lived with his wife and two small children. Dad and I looked at each other, and then Dad said, "Well, we'll pick some beans and I'll pay him."

In my own life in the city, things did not seem so extreme. It's true that sometimes when I came home from school Mother would be feeding a strange, ragged young man at the kitchen table. He had come and asked for food. Most people were quite willing to open their homes to these young men, whom we children called bums. We called them that because they had left their farm homes and "bummed" on the railways, stealing rides on freight cars, hoping to find jobs somewhere. They didn't want to be a burden to their families, who didn't have enough to feed the younger children, so they left. They were decent products of one-room schools and didn't arouse fear in anyone. If Mother thought the young man was in reasonably good health, she might ask him to mow the lawn or to sweep out the garage in exchange for his meal. If he looked sick, she might even take him down to the county hospital's emergency room. Older men who came to our door were treated the same way, but if Mother was worried about their being alcoholic, as some were, or bringing some disease germs into the house, she would bring their sandwiches to the back steps. There was a certain feeling in the days of the New Deal that everyone should pull together and try to help each other. Our doors were never locked.

Another consequence of the Depression was that I was not permitted to take care of children or do any other job which paid even 25 cents for the evening. My father said piously that these jobs must go to people who needed them more than I did. Some of my friends at U High were able to supplement their meager allowances with some of these neighborhood jobs. My father wouldn't even let my brothers be paperboys, although many of their friends earned money that way.

We rode the school bus to U High in the morning, and sometimes Mother gave us a ride; but we had to come home on the streetcar. Tokens for the streetcar were six for 45 cents, and it took two tokens to ride from Minneapolis, where U High was located, to St. Paul. It took me about an hour to get home and I had to transfer a couple of times. If I took the intercampus streetcar to the St. Paul university campus, it cost only three cents. Then I could use a token to take a streetcar to Snelling and Portland. The walk home was longer that way, but I saved two-and-a-half cents. If I had extra time, or the weather permitted a long walk, I chose that way.

My allowance was about one dollar a week, but that had to cover items like pencils, extra paper and a beverage at lunch if I decided to buy one. Mother packed us sandwiches, standing at the kitchen counter in her Hoover apron every morning before school. I usually drank water. If I managed to save two tokens and 35 cents from my allowance, which normally took more than a week—maybe as much as three or four weeks—I could then go downtown on Saturday afternoon with another girl on the streetcar, buy lunch at the Port Arthur Chinese Restaurant for 25 cents, and go to the movies at the Paramount Theater for 10 cents. Features in those days were short, but there was always a newsreel and a cartoon. There were no previews and the film showed continuously, so if we got there early, we would have time to watch it twice.

Clearly, the Depression was not as serious for my family as it was for many others. Still, I remember one time when my father was sitting on the piano bench and we had all been summoned to the living room to listen to him. He had helped his brother Allan and my mother's brother, Milford, start a company called Electrik Maid. They had found a patented electric oven that could be sold to bakeries, not to homes. Few bakeries and no individual families had that kind of equipment in the late 1920s when the company had started. Business had gone well at first, but we had heard that the three of them were not very satisfied with the manager they had hired. Of course, he traveled around to sell the ovens and reported in periodically to St. Paul. Milford lived in Chicago so he had left the company early. Much later, my father discovered that their manager had been embezzling. Starting this company had been one of my father's ideas of "helping" his younger brothers. During those Depression years, my father also sent checks to the widow of a cousin who was raising four sons. Since he managed Donny's investments, he sent her checks even when they didn't pay dividends.

That evening my father looked very solemn and said, "I have to tell you that the Electrik Maid is going bankrupt." He actually started to cry, and I had never seen him cry before. "I hope that I won't have to go personally bankrupt, but I might. I'm telling you because we might have to change everything about the way we live." I didn't understand what this meant. His crying amazed but didn't frighten me. I was astonished. I could see that my mother had been trying to stop my father from telling us all this, but I believe that he was not only afraid of what was coming, but that he also felt we children had to know what the real world was like. In fact he did not go bankrupt personally, and we heard little more about it. Electrik Maid was gone.

Even though he told us about this scare, we were not privy to information about his clients or his income. He never spoke about his law practice at home and considered it unethical ever to say anything about his clients. The most I ever heard, even when I was in senior high school, was, "Women have to know how to earn a living, because I've taken care of too many widows who were left with nothing after their husbands unexpectedly died. I have taken care of other widows who didn't know the first thing about managing their money and investments when their husbands had left them something. You have to get a good education and learn about these things."

From my mother I had learned about women's rights, women getting the vote, and birth control becoming legal. From my father I learned that I needed to know how to earn a living. This meant that I had to have a good education. My father never liked anything but A's on my report cards. He also seemed to give me an outlook more in touch with the later feminist movement of the 1960s than with women of my own generation, even though many of us went to work during World War II.

14

Mother and the German Refugees

My mother had told me that after we were all in high school, she wanted to look for a job. Maybe go back to teaching. She had long since given up her dream of going to medical school because in those days older people and women couldn't get in. My father had objected: if she went to work, people would think his law practice was failing and wouldn't come to him. She accepted the truth of this argument and kept on with her various volunteer efforts.

In the early 1930s, a few German-Jewish refugees began to come to St. Paul. When Jews arrived in New York at Ellis Island, they were sent by the Jewish agencies that received them to various communities in the United States according to the size of those places. It was considered undesirable to let all the refugees from Nazi Germany remain in New York. When this group began to arrive in St. Paul, my mother, working as a volunteer with Jewish Family Service, greeted them. She had the responsibility for helping them find apartments, jobs, and whatever services they might need. Although she didn't get paid,

Mother had her job.

She had "lined up" Jewish doctors and dentists to give free care to these people. She tried to find Jewish businessmen who would give them jobs, even the most menial ones, and if she could find a Jew who owned an apartment building, she would ask him for free or low-rent apartments for her new friends. It must be remembered that she was doing this during the Depression, when many American citizens were out of work and having difficulty paying for decent housing and medical care. Some of the men in the Jewish community were not sympathetic to her efforts, because they didn't want to be seen by Gentile customers, competitors, employees or renters as favoring "foreigners." Not only was there anti-Semitism, but also anyone coming from abroad was resented.

Before these people even arrived, I had seen my father sitting at the dining room table in the evening making out the affidavits that were required to bring German Jews to this country. At that time, the United States had made no provision for accepting people whose lives were endangered by the political situation in their own countries.

The law required that German Jews apply to the U.S. consular offices in their cities in Germany to get visas for coming to the United States. They had to enter the country under the German quota, which had been established by the immigration laws of 1924, even though Germany was systematically removing their rights as citizens. They had to prove that they were healthy, and they had to present affidavits—notarized promises from American citizens who were willing to prove that they could afford to support these people if they came to the United States. The U.S. citizen had to assure the government that the "aliens" would never be on public welfare after they arrived here. Even with all these affidavits, consular offices often simply refused to give visas.

My father began working on documents for my three cousins, the Horkheimers. He no longer went out to a meeting every night, but after dinner and his short nap, he would take his briefcase to the dining room table, dump out all the papers, and scowl over what he had found there. Sometimes he would mention to Mother that he had asked someone for an affidavit and had been refused. It was no light promise, during the Depression, to say that you would be responsible for a family or even an individual who might arrive with poor knowledge of English or with a profession like having been a lawyer in Germany that was of no use in the U.S.

In spite of the break with her Chicago relatives after her father had married Donny, Mother got in touch with them in order to help Jessie's children come to America. She had continued to correspond with her cousin since our visit to the Horkheimers in Frankfurt in 1929. Jessie's letters were censored, but once when she was visiting in Italy, she was able to write more clearly and said that there was no future for her children in Germany. She and Emil had decided to do everything possible to get them out. My father prepared the documents with affidavits from the wealthy Chicago family.

My cousin, Walter, was the first to arrive in the early thirties. He had to give up his ambitions and work as a stockboy in a Chicago warehouse, but he studied accounting in night school. Berni came next, taking a menial job and giving up his dreams of working in theater. They shared a tiny apartment.

That left Jessie, her husband Emil and Marianne in Germany. Emil was ill with MS and wouldn't be able to get an ordinary visa. However, Jessie discovered that if she came to the United States she could reclaim her American citizenship, which she had lost by marrying a national of another country. Then she could bring her husband and daughter. She came to the United States, but arrived back in Germany with cancer; she died in 1938, so the plan was void. Her citizenship was no help to her survivors. Marianne, a teenager, quietly applied for a visa for herself; her father clung to her as his illness got worse. They were together during "Kristallnacht" (the night of broken glass) hearing sirens everywhere and assurances on the radio that firefighters would protect German buildings while Jewish homes, businesses, and synagogues were burned. They heard reports that Emil's building and property were totally destroyed, everything from typewriters to bolts of cloth thrown out the windows and stolen or burned. Then the building itself was wrecked. Later, men came to their home, tore books, took everything of value, destroyed what they didn't want, but didn't take her father to a concentration camp because he looked too old and sick.

After that night he reluctantly gave Marianne permission to leave, and she arrived in New York in 1939. She learned later that her father had been taken to a concentration camp where he perished.

I was at Vassar College by then and met her in New York. She was brave and proud and didn't want to speak about her humiliating and terrifying experiences. I learned her story much later.

At age twelve, Marianne had to sit in the back row in her German school. A year later she was expelled for being Jewish.

For a while, she attended a school set up by the Jewish community and then went to a Jewish hospital where she worked and learned to be a medical technician. In Chicago she stayed with a cousin and worked at Michael Reese Hospital. She told me years later that she spent most of her time on the roof of the hospital injecting rabbits with urine from women to find out whether they were pregnant or not. Apparently she also had to kill the rabbits to get the results. She worried about her father and heard nothing about him after the war started. The Horkheimer kids came to Bone Lake a few times for vacations, and Marianne and I became close. Berni and Walter were too old for my brothers and didn't especially appreciate a place without plumbing and electricity.

My mother felt at home with Jewish people from Germany. She was truly bilingual, and was flattered when they asked her what town she had come from in Germany. She shared with them a love of German "Kultur"— Goethe, Heine, Beethoven and Brahms, to name a few. Before 1939, when Germany invaded Poland, she had found it difficult to believe that the German people were in agreement with Hitler.

Mother was disappointed that I couldn't speak German with these new friends when she invited them to our home. Dream daughter would have been as fluent as she was, but I was suffering from a particularly difficult teacher of German at U High. The Fräulein was a "native speaker," and as soon as I started to study with her it became clear that she sympathized with Hitler. She said he was making German youth brave and strong, he was revitalizing the economy, etc. I liked it when she taught us German songs but felt miserable when she told one of the boys that he "had a yellow streak up and down his back like most

Americans." Her contempt for Americans in general and Jews in particular became more clear as the next years went by. She said she could always tell a Jew because he had a Yiddish accent and couldn't learn proper German.

For me there was no love of German culture. Probably what stopped me from learning what little she was teaching was the advent of a practice teacher who had studied at Heidelberg. Because his face was severely scarred from dueling with swords, she held him up to us as a great example of German manhood. German students thought it macho to duel without masks. The two of them spoke together in German and ignored the class altogether.

When Mother invited many of the refugees for dinner, I realized how much they appreciated her warmth and her sympathy. They preferred to speak English anyway because they were eager to learn. I was proud that she was carrying out her belief that those who were educated and well-off should help others who were less privileged. Many of the German Jews who came were indeed well-educated. She helped one attorney get a scholarship to study political science at the university. After he got his Ph.D., he taught in some fine colleges on the West Coast. One young man had learned to be a baker and she found him a job, too. On Grand Avenue, near Fairview, there was a bakery called Koenig's. Koenig means king in German; my father sometimes teased Mrs. Koenig, who waited on customers, by calling her "Die Koenigen," or "the queen." She was a shy little woman and easily embarrassed, but I believe this German couple hired Mother's Jewish baker.

I remember one day when Mother came home really breathing fire. She had sent a young mother with her baby to a Jewish pediatrician. He had found the child somewhat malnourished and had told the mother she should give the baby bacon because it had vitamin B. The woman was horrified; she kept kosher. My mother was waiting for this doctor to come home so she could call him up and "give him hell." Her expression surprised me, since she seldom swore. Pretty soon I heard her on the telephone telling him that he had no business prescribing bacon to any Jewish patients unless he first inquired whether they were observant or not. Before she had finished, it was clear that he was going to call the woman and change his orders. Of course, Mother added later, speaking to us, this young mother would take anything the doctor told her as the absolute law, even though she was crying when she told Mother about it. I understood, because my mother also tended to take the words of authorities like doctors as binding. My father was a little looser in that respect. The irony was that Mother not only didn't keep kosher but also thought it was irrelevant to the Jewish religion.

One young man arrived from Germany with a back injury. He had been beaten in a concentration camp, for no reason that he knew, and then let go. Although Mother got him medical help, his injury was permanent. She got him a menial job that accommodated the injury. His new boss persuaded him to shorten his German name into something more like an English one. This angered my mother because she said it made the man feel embarrassed and uncomfortable to change his name. To this day his daughter lives in Minneapolis and tells me how much her parents appreciated the help my mother gave them.

At one point a number of young Jewish men were living at

an old Civilian Conservation Corps (CCC) camp near Shakopee. The CCC was one of the New Deal agencies; camps were set up in state and national parks and young men were employed doing conservation work, such as planting trees, building trails, etc. The camp near Shakopee was no longer in use. Most of the Jewish boys were in their late teens and both the St. Paul and Minneapolis communities were finding homes for them to live in with Jewish families or trying to get them enrolled in the University of Minnesota. Some of them later lived and worked at Jewish fraternities. Among these young men was one who later became chancellor of the University of Minnesota at Moorhead, and another who became chancellor of the state college system in Minnesota. But while I was in high school, they were not much older than I was, and their futures were very cloudy. Their families were still in danger. One of these young men went to live with my husband-to-be in his home in Minneapolis. Another lived with another family that we knew in St. Paul.

Much to my surprise, my father did not want my mother to bring one of these adolescents into our home to live. He said they could visit in town or at the lake, and she could feed them as often as she wanted, but that was it. When I questioned him, he said vehemently, "Practice charity. Give money. Help people. Volunteer. But don't give charity in your very own home." Again I asked him why. And then he reminded me that although he had had his own bedroom when he was a boy, he seldom got to sleep in it because his parents were always bringing home relatives from Europe. Unlike in the Depression era, immigration had been easy when Dad was a boy.

My mother's strong belief and practice that Jews must help

each other and that those with privileges must help the less privileged, no matter who they were, was not original with her. My father's parents, with their house like Noah's Ark, had behaved the same way. I learned about the experiences of people from many places and situations different from my own. I was thoroughly indoctrinated with the idea that I had major obligations to others.

15

Camping

When I was fourteen, Mother decided I could go to a somewhat more rigorous camp called Camp Holiday, which specialized in canoe trips and other outdoor adventure activities. I enjoyed learning to set up a wilderness camp in the Boundary Waters with a minimum of equipment, and to canoe, portage, and camp out, not just overnight, but for three or four days. My U High School friend Cherrie was also there, which made it more pleasant than having to make all new friends.

My mother was a great believer in camping. For many years she was the chairman of Sophie Wirth Camp, established in the early 1920s at White Bear Lake, primarily to serve disadvantaged Jewish children. However, since it was the only kosher camp in the Upper Midwest at that time, it attracted children from middle-class Orthodox families. Every summer there were separate twelve-day periods for young boys, young girls, older boys, older girls, and one for mothers with preschool children.

My mother managed this camp for many years, hiring the staff, supervising the maintenance of the buildings and grounds, establishing programs, making sure that the camp was totally kosher, and ensuring that it was safe and enjoyable. She belonged to the American Camping Association and was very knowledgeable about all aspects of camping. The camp program was similar to Scout or Y camps. It had an infirmary—always manned by a senior medical student; the swimming program was directly supervised by the Red Cross.

There was a big two-story frame lodge painted dark green, with a kitchen, a large living room and screened porches where campers ate their meals. Upstairs were dormitory rooms; there was a separate building with a concrete floor for toilets and showers. The plumber was a friend and client of my father's; most of his service was gratis. Over the years, extra land was acquired for more cabins—one for arts and crafts, another for the director to live in, and a couple to house additional campers. The beach was separated from the buildings by the railroad track, which ran along the north side of White Bear Lake. This made the swimming period especially fun, because everyone had to parade across the tracks when no trains were coming. The beach became a special place where one couldn't go easily. The camp also had rowboats and canoes.

For years I had gone with my parents to visit Sophie Wirth, often on the way to Bone Lake, so that Mother could make her inspections and solve any unusual problems.

One of Mother's many jobs was to raise money for this camp. Every year all of the members of the Council of Jewish Women and their families were invited to come out for a picnic, bringing their own food. My father would order the cooks—overweight Mrs. Goren and tiny, birdlike Mrs. Nymark—to bake many loaves of bread. He would supply them with a few gold coins to bake in some of the loaves. After the people had eaten, he would auction off every loaf of bread with the enticement that some of them contained gold coins, besides being the most delicious, home-baked, kosher bread available anywhere in the whole world. Apparently this tactic was quite successful, although I know that there were many other fundraising efforts as well. Parents of campers who were able paid the fees, but others paid nothing.

The children were examined prior to going to camp by doctors who donated their time. They met at the Central Community House, of which my mother was board president. Occasionally the doctors would find a problem that required medical treatment, which was then provided by whatever means were available. Most often, children were found with head lice. There was loud screaming when children thought they couldn't go to camp, but they were sent home with instructions to rub kerosene on their scalps and then to shampoo. Usually the treatment was effective and the child was accepted for camp. Many children gained weight in camp, a matter which was carefully recorded. Those who were seriously underweight were given milk and crackers between meals and at night before bed.

One year, when somehow the menus had escaped my mother's all-seeing eyes, the cooks served Jell-O after a dairy meal. Kosher rules require that milk and meat products not be served together. The children at Sophie Wirth were well aware that the gelatin in Jell-O was a meat product. A food riot ensued; red Jell-O was thrown all over the dining room—all over everybody's hair, all over everybody's clothes, the tables, and the floor. It apparently took the director, Mrs. Zack, a long time to calm the kids down and even longer to clean up. When my mother heard about it, she was appalled—not only that the children rioted—but that the cooks, both of whom claimed to keep kosher at home, had made the Jell-O in the first place. It is really ironic that my mother was the one to enforce these rules. She wanted to serve the poor mothers who needed vacations, and the Jewish children who were living in the slums of St. Paul and Minneapolis, and who had no opportunity to experience camping, the natural world, or the healthy life of swimming and hiking. To do this she became an expert at kashrut, in spite of her own feelings.

After my senior year in high school, I went to Sophie Wirth to be a counselor during the girls' period. My charges were mostly nine years old, including one little girl who had a rather serious case of asthma. I went there with the idea that as a graduate of all those different camps I would have a lot to teach the children. What they taught me was Yiddishkeit, which was more valuable to me than anything I taught them. They knew how to make jokes about their misfortunes; they knew a lot of funny little Yiddish sayings, which they were surprised they had to translate for me. I learned some colorful Yiddish words; they taught me many Yiddish songs. I learned about "Shabbos."

On Friday night, everyone who was able to wore white clothes, or at least a white shirt. We had an especially good dinner, always chicken, and braided bread, challah. Candles were blessed and lit at every table, a blessing was offered over bread and grape juice, and everyone entered into the spirit of the Sabbath. At home, Friday night had meant my parents going off to temple. As I grew older, I sometimes joined them. But Friday night at camp turned out to be not a serious Jewish moment, but a joyful one. Saturday activities, after outdoor services, were much quieter and more relaxed than the rest of the week. I had a taste of a different kind of Judaism from what my parents practiced, and it appealed to me.

Most of the counselors and the director were Jewish people who were attending the University of Minnesota or had graduated. In the evenings we would get together to discuss any problems we were having with our little charges. It must be remembered that these children came from homes of poverty. Most of their parents were foreign-born. Nevertheless, our director—no longer Mrs. Zack but a younger woman—was some kind of an amateur psychologist. She attributed all the children's behavior problems to over-protective, over-indulgent mothers. As I think back about how ridiculous this was, when all of these mothers were struggling—many of them working outside of the home, doing housework under primitive conditions and trying to take care of big families—I realize how we apply stereotypes to ourselves as well as to others.

Romances occasionally blossomed among the staff, and I even had one date. On my day off, the medical counselor took me to Wildwood, the amusement park at Mahtomedi. He was quite a few years older than I, and I wonder if he might have taken me on a bet. Anyway, he took me on my first and last roller coaster ride. I felt so sick afterwards that I didn't mind not having any more dates the rest of the summer.

Sophie Wirth Camp continued until World War II made it impossible to recruit staff. Most of the children of these "over-protective, overindulgent" mothers managed to get good educations and become professional or middle-class people, many of them getting their educations on the G.I. Bill after serving in World War II.

16

Senior Year at U High

The two women who were most important to me my senior year were Mrs. Wettleson, the journalism teacher and girls' advisor, and our maid, Ann Johansen. Both were Norwegians, both tall, with faded blonde hair, pale blue eyes and little snub noses. Sometimes in odd moments you could even hear a lilt in their voices not usually heard in English. Both were American born, both came from farms, and both were very intelligent in spite of the difference in their formal educations. One of the differences in appearance was that Mrs. Wettleson had a clear complexion while Ann had a face severely scarred from acne. Sometimes, even though she was in her late twenties, new outbreaks would occur. My mother had paid for her to visit our skin doctor, who helped with the new pimples but could do nothing about the scars. Ann tried to wear makeup to cover them. She always wore a maid's uniform, blue, pink or white, and a white apron.

Mrs. Wettleson was in her thirties, wore dark skirts and washable blouses to school, and had an air of authority about her. She was putting her husband through graduate school, hoping they would someday follow his career rather than hers. Mrs. Wettleson was an effective, no-nonsense teacher in the class I took from her my senior year, a combination of journalism and English. She was the adviser to the *Campus Breeze*, so I had known her through the years as I wrote and did some editing for the paper. She was also the adviser to girls; if I needed an excuse to skip gym or a request to leave school to go to some event on campus, such as a convocation, to report for the *Breeze*, I went to her for my pink slip to hand the classroom teacher.

Ann, our maid since I was eight years old, worked according to her own version of the Lutheran no-nonsense work ethic. She was efficient and thorough and didn't want me hanging around her kitchen. Yet sometimes when she had finished the task at hand, she and I had friendly talks. She would talk about her hard life on the farm. It was my mother who told me that Ann's father was an alcoholic who expected his many children to do the work on his subsistence farm. Ann told me her mother was a sister of a certain famous Norwegian writer, but because their farm was so poor and they had so many children, Ann had had to quit the one-room school she attended in fourth grade to stay home and help with the younger kids. She showed me a picture of her sister's little girl, about five years old, and said she was saving to help that child get the education that had been denied her. I held her hand and there were tears in my eyes—it was so easy for me to go to school. I felt like an ingrate for not appreciating being a senior at U High.

The year started out with a terrible disappointment. All my years at U High, I had wanted to be editor of the *Breeze* when I was a senior. I was the best writer in the class, I thought, and I had worked on the newspaper since junior high. I had decided that a classmate, Don Reilly, could be sports editor, because I had never been to a single sports event in my high school career. No one ever asked me, for one thing, and I had therefore decided I wasn't interested. Anyway, I told myself, U High lost almost every game they ever played.

Don was a redhead with a strong profile and a pleasant manner; I thought he was more civilized than a lot of the boys and I knew he was interested in journalism.

My brother George had been editor of the *Breeze* the previous year. He had no big interest in writing, and I'm not sure how he got the job—which was a faculty decision—no election or anything. He published a few of his own cartoons, kept the staff going, and had done a reasonable job. The *Breeze* office was a small room with a desk, a typewriter and a few shelves with old "cuts"—etched metal plates attached to blocks of wood, the method of printing illustrations in those days. The paper was set in linotype by a commercial printer. Making new cuts was expensive, so trying to find a wisecrack sort of headline to put under an old picture was one of our frequent projects to fill an odd space—George had been good at that.

In my high school years I had become more like Mother: I was an officer of the Girls' Club (all the girls in the school), Acme (the Girls' Honor Society), as well as Quill and Scroll (writers, of course). I did publicity for the music department's annual Gilbert and Sullivan operetta (George had a part in "Pirates of Penzance"), and I planned the banquet for the Latin Club ("wear your toga"). If I wasn't tall and strong, at least I was somebody important in the school and doing the kind of volunteer work available, and so becoming more like Mother's dream daughter. Mother and I could talk over how to run committee meetings and our disappointment with and moral superiority to those who promised and didn't deliver. We had things in common.

By ninth grade I had my special girlfriends with whom I continued to have lunch every day at Shevlin. The group changed sometimes, but six or seven of us were at the core and we talked about school spirit and our favorite songs ("Smoke Gets In Your Eyes" or "Deep Purple"), movie stars, and the girls we disliked the most, who sat at the other end of the lunch room. They were a club, they said, called FAF—the meaning of the initials was a secret. Theoretically U High had no sororities, but these girls, who were the cheerleaders and got whatever dates there were, behaved like a sorority. They were known to us as Fast American Females. We were better students; we were sure they had more fun. We pretended to hate them and told each other it was best to ignore them. But of course we were full of envy.

I even had two special friends, Rosemary and Cherrie, with whom I had formed for a joke "The Ancient and Honorable Society of Man Haters." When we ate by ourselves we thought up hilarious things to say about the dumb boys in our classes. I was convinced that most boys were stupider than most girls.

The first day of my senior year, Mrs. Wettleson called me into her plain small office, with its one window, a sad geranium on the sill, a battered wooden desk, and a chair facing it. She was sitting behind her desk, smiling, but with her chin somehow sticking out in a determined way at the same time. She told me to sit down.

"I'm pleased to tell you that you've been elected to National Honor Society on the basis of your grades," she said, "although this won't be announced till the end of the quarter."

"Thanks," I said, not surprised because my grades were better than some people who had been elected last spring. Mother had explained that since George had been elected the previous spring as a senior, it wasn't right for me to be elected the same year as a junior. I could wait till I was a senior. I had gulped and started to cry and run from the room. I had worked so hard. I had better grades. My brother always had fun, and I didn't.

The previous spring Mother had felt sorry for me and invited a bunch of kids to my house for my birthday. Except she hadn't told me. I came home about five o'clock on May 5th, out of sorts because no one had mentioned my birthday that morning, and when I walked in the house kids had popped out from behind the chairs and the sofa and yelled, "Surprise!" There I was in my old school clothes and they had presents and Mother and Ann served supper, but somehow I didn't like being surprised and wished she had told me...and let me do some of the planning. She and Ann were around the whole time and Dad showed up too, and my brothers. *Watching us, like watching the monkeys in the zoo,* I thought.

"And there's something else." Mrs. Wettleson was smiling that nonsmile again. "You have been selected to be associate editor of the *Breeze* this year."

"I thought I'd be editor," I blurted out. "Haven't I worked more than anybody?"

"You have worked hard," she said, "but your mother and I consulted about this. We both felt you had a very heavy schedule this year, and she tells me that you have been complaining of a pain in your side, so we felt—and your brother George agreed—that the editorship would be too much for you. Don Reilly will be editor and he will need your help and I know he will appreciate it."

"Don Reilly?" I collapsed in the chair. I put my hands over my face. I couldn't say anything. I felt angry, betrayed, let down, but I wasn't crying. I finally looked up at her. "Maybe I won't do it at all!" I said defiantly, "You can look for somebody else." I knew there wasn't anyone as qualified as I was. Was it because he was a boy?

"I understand how you feel," she retained her Scandinavian calm, "but we've never had an associate editor before—only assistant editors. It's a good title. You will have an important job. It'll look good on your college application. So think it over."

"That's all?" I asked. She nodded.

My first day of classes included second-year Latin, so I could qualify to go away to a good college and get away from this place, physics (which I liked, although there were only two girls in the class), gym, which I hated most of all, social studies (economics), and Mrs. W's journalism class. I felt like skipping it, but I didn't—just sat in the back and never raised my hand. Senior year was going to be the pits. I knew it would be spiteful to give up my ambition, but I felt a failure, betrayed. I couldn't talk it over with Mother either. She was a big part of my problem.

When I got home from school that afternoon Ann said, "Your mother will be home at five o'clock."

"That's what you always say," I grumbled.

She looked me over and asked, "What's the matter? You want something to eat?" I sat down at the kitchen table and she handed me an apple and put a cookie on a plate.

"I don't know what to do." I told her about Mrs. Wettleson. "Should I be associate editor or just chuck it?" By the time I finished I was crying.

She patted my back and took a hanky out of my purse and handed it to me. I sobbed my thanks.

"Your mother's a smart woman," she said, "and you do get tired all the time and talk about that pain in your side."

"It's not all the time," I defended myself, "just sometimes…"

"Half a loaf is better than none," she told me. She never got to go to high school. She had to work long hours in people's houses. She was going to try to get her little niece through high school.

"I know," I said. "You had to go to town to get away from the farm and when I leave, Mom says you can go to beauty school and get a better job, so that's your half a loaf."

"Yah."

I went up to my room with my pile of books. Mom was busy with her refugees and Sophie Wirth Camp; Dad was always busy. The boys were both away now, Linn at Harvard Law School and George at Harvard College. I was angry and lonely and felt no one cared about me… All I could think of was how great it would be to go away to college. But what college would take me? I wouldn't know till April—and it was now only September—and who would help me with the applications? Senior year loomed, black as midnight.

I couldn't get out of gym, even as a senior. One more year of the smelly locker room and the smelly black bloomers we had to wear with white middy blouses. No matter how often I took them home to launder, they always seemed to stink. I hated taking showers without curtains or separating walls so the other girls could see my little stomach and my flat feet. Some practice teacher (a senior in the Department of Education who was teaching her first classes) once more decided she could cure my flat feet with exercises, even though it hadn't worked in ninth, tenth or eleventh grade, and I told her so. It didn't do any good.

Senior year a practice teacher discovered I could swim and another practice teacher, a wiry brunette, decided to teach me to do a back dive. I stood on the edge of the board with my back to the pool and my hands on her shoulders. She had her hands on my waist and told me to bend backwards. I froze. She talked. The other girls and the regular teacher watched. I smelled the chlorine. I couldn't move. Stalemate. Finally, thinking she was pushing me, I dove in, stung my shoulders and never tried it again.

They taught me to put my head in the water and breathe with my breaststroke and I was sent to a girls' swimming meet at The College of St. Catherine in St. Paul. I lost my race.

Many days after school Don and I worked in the *Breeze* office trying to put a four-page paper together. I began to notice how his upper lip quivered when he was excited about something. I thought he was very handsome. After a month or two I began to imagine that he would take me out on a date or maybe to a game or a sock hop. He didn't. He was capable and businesslike and not unkind, while I was sure I was falling in love with him. But I could never let on. Not for one second. Instead, I dealt with the printers, wrote news stories and features, and edited the work of others. I learned to count type in order to write formal or ragged headlines. By the time I finished high school, I knew basic journalism.

In the late fall, after conferring with two different doctors, it was decided that I had appendicitis. My parents took me to St. Joseph's Hospital where, to my disgust, I was put in the pediatric ward. The nuns said I was only fifteen, and you had to be sixteen to be with the adults. When the nuns weren't around, the kids raced wheelchairs up and down the halls, which smelled of disinfectant. The day before the surgery I was in a room with three small children who cried half the night.

Mother asked the doctor if she could watch the surgery, explaining that she had always been interested in medicine. He agreed. Afterwards I was happy to have a room to myself. While I fought my way out of the anesthesia, Mother told me I had a layer of yellow fat under my skin, just like a chicken. I was less than delighted. I was five feet tall and weighed 110 pounds, but I was convinced I was too fat. Mother's report didn't help. The surgeon said my appendix hadn't been infected, but had grown around the intestine in an unusual way. The pain in my side didn't go away, a medical mystery for several years until it was found to be diverticulitis.

A few days after the surgery, I was sitting up in my white bed in my white hospital room with the crucifix behind my head (where I didn't have to look at it), when several girls from school crowded into my room. First Rosemary handed me a large package saying, "Everybody loves this book, and now that you're sitting around the hospital you'll have time to read it."

They watched while I tore off the white tissue paper and found *Gone with the Wind*. I thanked them and immediately realized the book was so heavy I'd have a hard time holding it away from my sore belly.

One of them informed me that Pug Lund, the Golden Gopher star football player, was practice-teaching in second hour social studies. "He's really handsome," she told me, "and all the girls are trying to get him to notice them. But he's very serious."

Cherrie said, "We've got a cute blonde named Miss Hanson in English and Tom asked her for a date!"

Everybody started to giggle. "What did she say?" I asked.

She mimicked a high soprano voice, "You'll have to wait a few years, dearie."

I started to laugh, too, and it hurt my stomach. "Don't make me laugh," I pleaded, "just tell me what else is going on while I'm here."

Lorraine started, "Well, the photographer…" but immediately the other girls began going "shhh."

"What photographer?" I knew it was bad news…

Rosemary spoke up. "You'd find out sooner or later anyway, but Mrs. Wettleson did tell us not to let you know yet…" Rosemary was the art editor of the school annual.

"For the *Bisbila*?" I asked weakly. She nodded. So my picture would be missing from the school annual, my senior year when I should have been in Girls Club, Acme, Quill and Scroll, National Honor, Latin club, *Breeze*… "Oh no," I groaned.

"Your class picture in the front of the book will have a list of everything you've accomplished," Cherrie said primly.

"Thanks a lot," I said. "And have they taken all the pictures by now?" I was hoping maybe a few remained.

"He's all done," they told me.

I got home from the hospital, made up my school work and started a column for the *Breeze* called "Will O' the Whisper." It was a great title for a gossip column that I had invented myself, but I had to gather the gossip from other girls. It seldom seemed to come my way.

My brothers came home for Christmas vacation and Dad immediately announced that we'd go up to Bone Lake for a weekend. There was plenty of snow for skiing. We usually went in late January to watch Mr. Anderson cut ice for our icehouse. He'd take his team out on the lake with an open sled, saw big hunks of ice, tip them out of the lake with huge tongs, and then one of his sons would help him lift them onto the sled with another set of tongs. The blocks weighed more than a hundred pounds each. Dad would have ordered a load of sawdust from a small lumber mill and had it dumped by the icehouse in the fall. The men, stuffed into their wool clothes, snowpacs and knitted hats, moved like bears trying to walk on two legs. Their breath poured out like steam into the bitterly cold clear air. But they'd get the chore done, and because I was watching, they would only swear under their steaming breath.

Layers of ice and layers of sawdust were loaded into our icehouse. They would last all summer. Christmas was too early to cut ice and Dad said with a chuckle that this year he'd let Mr. Anderson do it on his own. In the earlier years we had parked our car at a garage in Milltown and Mr. Anderson had picked us up with his team. The horses had bells on their harnesses, and the sled was piled with straw and some coarse horse blankets. We went on deep snow over fields and fences directly to our place. When the snow prevented us from opening the doors, the farmer had helped Dad dig our way in.

By 1936 the township roads were regularly plowed and because Dad got up and started the car religiously, it didn't freeze up, but got us back to town.

My sweaters, wool pants, wool coat, hats and mittens from the previous year all fit me; so did the snowpacs. We all wore long, slightly scratchy underwear. Coming up in the car was like old times; Dad was in a great mood, joking about his over-educated sons. He even abandoned his smelly cigar when I asked him to because the car windows were closed.

When we got to the cabin, we went about our chores like a good team, the boys shoveling the paths to the pump and the outhouse, Dad opening the shutters, Mother and I heating water on the stove to prime the pump (the water was frozen in the pail), sweeping out the poisoned wheat and a couple of dead mice, shaking the mothballs out of the extra blankets and bringing the cots from the porch into the living room. Dad had put an airtight stove in front of the fireplace the previous fall. Now he brought in the wood he and the boys had split and started the fire. The air was stale and cold; soon we had hot faces when we stood by the stove, but cold behinds. The room warmed up slowly and we opened one window a little for fresh air. When we complained too much of the cold Dad offered us a sip of whiskey.

Once the stove was going, the place was open, and the food unloaded from the car, we all went to the hill.

George went down to the boathouse and got our yellow pine Northland skis with black straps that went over our boots, and our poles. We hiked up the side of the hill with the skis on our shoulders and slid down. He announced that the fellows at Harvard had told him about ski harnesses that kept your foot firmly on the ski and enabled you to steer down a hill and even to climb back up. He hoped to buy a pair.

We laughed to watch Dad skiing down the hill smoking his pipe. George tried a snowplow turn that his friends had told him about and fell off the skis into the snow; Linn looked graceful. I loved the feeling of sliding, gliding, almost flying down that hill. Even though drops were freezing on my eyelashes, I sweated, climbing back up. It was worth it for the exhilarating slide all the way down.... Our parents went back to the cabin, but we stayed until the sun began to go down and the temperature dropped. Then we, too, trudged back.

Mother had hot cocoa ready, and chicken reheated that Ann had cooked at home, and good Swedish rye from the Lindstrom Bakery, where we always stopped on the way up, and plenty of other things to eat, too. We talked about plans for the next day—there was too much snow on the lake to skate across, but we could ski or hike, and Dad had phoned Mrs. Tony to have dinner ready for us tomorrow at one o'clock. Mr. and Mrs. Tony had a farm, but they had once owned a Bohemian restaurant in Chicago where Mrs. Tony had been the chef. She would fix a delicious heavy dinner for us if forewarned.

That night I slept in my long johns and a sweater, curled up as tightly as an unopened peony bud. I tried to keep the blanket over my head, except for my nose, which I knew was red. But I slept wonderfully and woke happy to watch Dad stoking the fire in the stove and Mother checking the big battered aluminum teakettle to see if the water was still hot so she could wash at the kitchen sink. I would skip that for today and no one would complain.

The boys started jumping around in their long johns, yelling that the Pater Familias was trying to freeze them to death, and we were all laughing, which is a fine way to warm up. I loved George again, as I always would after that. Our conflicts in high school no longer mattered. All I wanted to do was finish and get away to college.

It was a great time, and then suddenly the boys were gone again and I was back at school, "the grind," we all called it. A new counselor who had just been added to the staff at U High was helping me fill out college applications. He told me mine looked good—I was one of the top students in my class and had a lot of extra-curricular activities. My parents had decided I should go to a girls' college because they thought I was too young for a co-ed school. I couldn't imagine anything more wonderful than having boys out of my hair. I wanted, I yearned, I longed for Don Reilly to think I was a girl, take me out on a date, but I was convinced he only thought of me as a workhorse. Even though the girls did better in classes, the boys got all the jobs—editor of the paper, class officers, captains of sports teams, the best roles in the class play. It was so unfair!

I applied to Wellesley, Mount Holyoke, and Vassar. But I wanted Vassar because I wanted to be a writer, and I knew that Edna St. Vincent Millay had gone there. All I knew about the colleges was what I read in their catalogues, and they all sounded good. There was no money to go and visit and no effort was made by the schools to have me meet alumnae, if there were any in the Twin Cities. Mother had gone to Vassar, but she was sure it had changed a lot since she graduated in 1907.

I was living through senior year joylessly when Mother got an acute attack of arthritis and was sent to the hospital. It was frightening to see her in bed there, with one leg in traction, which didn't help her at all. I could see the pain on her face, even though she didn't complain. The doctors decided she had abscessed teeth and two were pulled—that made her look worse, of course. I had never seen my mother powerless before, nor had I ever imagined that she would get old and change. Even though she had told me stories of her childhood that were sad, I hadn't really felt sorry for her. Now I did. Now I began to realize that bigger changes than going away to college might be coming in my life. I knew I wasn't ready.

Mother got home from the hospital, still with a lot of pain in her back; she had difficulty walking. The next part of the prescription was to take her to a warm place; late in February, she and Dad departed for three weeks in Mexico.

Now Ann and I were alone. I'd walk in from school and the house wouldn't even smell good—what was the point of baking pie or roasting meat for two people? We would sit in the kitchen and have supper together and not always know what to talk about. I bottled up my complaints about Don Reilly and the girls of FAF and the printer being late with the page proofs. She kept the house clean, received the laundry mailed home by the boys, and returned it clean and carefully ironed in the special boxes bought from the post office with a card that was turned weekly, one side addressed to our house and one side addressed to a brother. Sometimes she baked on Saturdays so she could send them cookies with the laundry and then we'd have some, too.

My postconfirmation class at Mt. Zion met on Sunday mornings to discuss comparative religion. We also visited church services, which I found interesting intellectually, but also uncomfortable. I'd been to mass with Agnes, my friend on the block, all in Latin, of course, so I could mostly observe the pageantry without absorbing any ideas. Now we went to a few different Protestant churches. I recognized the psalms and some of the other prayers that were much like ours, but sometimes when I heard "in Jesus's name," an involuntary shiver went through me as I remembered all the persecutions and pogroms, the Inquisition, wondering about the Nazis in Germany, not understanding the connections between these benign Christian services and the people who greeted us cordially afterwards, kindly offering to answer our questions, and the anti-Semitism I knew existed not only in the past but also at the present time in Minnesota. I didn't dare ask our hosts or hostesses about anti-Semitism, nor did the teacher who was with us, or any of my classmates. The truth was I didn't want to think about it.

Dad and Mother came home; Mother was considerably improved and found a new doctor in Minneapolis who seemed to be helping her. She wore a huge device, called a Camp Corset, with stays and laces, and said it braced her up and helped her walk. I was reassured by her resumed attitude of being in charge.

Senior prom loomed as a crisis—I already knew Don was taking one of the FAF girls. Most of the girls I lunched with at Shevlin admitted they had dates. I didn't. Mother knew it. Saturday afternoon the week before the prom I got a phone call. A boy in my class, whose mother was a friend of my mother.

He was blunt. "I wasn't gonna go to the senior prom," he told me, "but my mother said it would be fun, so do you want to go?"

I didn't. My face was red. Our mothers had arranged it and I didn't even like this boy. He was too tall and if I danced with him, my face would be up against the buttons on his vest. But what would I say? Obviously he had asked other girls and they had refused. Why else would he call so late?

"Ruth? Did you hear me?"

"Yah, thanks," I said. "Sure, okay, I'll go."

"I'll pick you up at seven then," he said and hung up.

The awful part was that Mother was listening and smiling benignly. She thought I'd be happy! "Do we need to buy you a long dress?" she asked.

"Yeah, a formal…if they make them my size," I added. "I know you arranged it!"

"You'll have fun," she told me.

But I didn't. My date danced with other girls, and few boys asked me. Don Reilly never even noticed I was there. I spilled food on my dress and was embarrassed. It was the wrong dress anyway—everybody was in slinky skirts and mine was full. I was a wallflower. I had been taught to waltz, but nobody was waltzing, and I stepped on somebody's foot. All night long I was embarrassed. At least when my date brought me home he made no effort to kiss me. I had been worried about that all night. What was I supposed to do if he tried? He just touched my shoulder and said "goodnight."

Senior year was almost over when I got wonderful news: I was admitted to both Mount Holyoke and Vassar, and I quickly wrote back that I would come to Vassar. Emancipation! I would get away and be on my own!

Behind the curtain in Scott Hall on graduation day, all of us in black caps and gowns, Don Reilly stood next to me for a minute. Would he at least touch me, put his hand on my shoulder, say he'd miss me, thank me for working with him? He sighed. "They say these are the best years of our lives," he said, "and now they're over."

I was so aghast, I couldn't think of a thing to say to him.

17

College and Marriage

When I was sixteen, in the fall of 1937, I set off for Vassar College by train. There were three fast trains to Chicago—the *Zephyr*, the *Hiawatha*, and the *400* ("400 miles in 400 minutes"). It was exciting to enter the huge, high Union Depot with my family to board the train. My steamer trunk was checked through and I sat in the coach by myself watching the scenery go by until I got to Chicago. Since this was my first time traveling alone, my parents had arranged for my uncle Milford to meet me. He helped me with my hand luggage and explained to me the works of the Parmelee vans, which took passengers from one railway station to another. I had come in on the Chicago-Milwaukee & St. Paul Railroad and would continue my journey on the New York Central.

In the station I saw a familiar redheaded man with his tall, lanky, redheaded son. I hadn't seen them since I was nine or ten, but because we had to pass by, I knew I must introduce them to my uncle. My father had two redheaded friends, Henry Weiller and Arthur Brin; I wasn't sure which one this was. Both had teenage sons. I introduced my uncle and used the name Henry Weiller. To my immense embarrassment, Mr. Brin said, "Of course, Mr. Weiller and I are often confused, but I'm Arthur Brin and this is my son, Howard." I know I was blushing and feeling miserable, as I always did in these overpowering social situations. The two men exchanged a few jovial remarks, and we were on our way. Yet this was a portentous meeting because of events to follow. Milford got me to the New York Central, I slept overnight on the Pullman, and arrived at the Poughkeepsie station the next morning.

I was met by a "big sister," a sophomore from Vassar assigned to help freshmen like me. My trunk and I were put in a taxi and installed in a room in Main, the oldest building on the Vassar campus. I would share the room with an assigned roommate whom I had never met. This girl's name was Janet, and she came to school with a group of friends from her prep school on the East Coast. Except that we slept in the same room, I saw very little of her. Although she was unfriendly, I really didn't notice much because I was totally submerged in keeping up with my classes. The campus was beautiful. I was vastly relieved to be with girls; boys and dates were forgotten. My classes were exciting and I was meeting girls from all over—from foreign students to preppies.

My classes were zoology, political science, English, and beginning French. My German teacher at U High had been so inadequate and so fond of the Nazis that I knew I couldn't manage an intermediate German course. What I didn't realize was that many of the girls in my French class had either had French governesses, spent a few months in France, or possibly taken a semester of French somewhere along the line. I was a total beginner. It was much more difficult for me than any of the other subjects. I loved zoology and political science and found English very easy. The girls who had gone to prep schools had much better backgrounds in English literature than I did, but Mark Twain and Walt Whitman were new to them, while I had already begun reading them in high school.

After about six weeks, I came to my room one day to find my roommate Janet packing. She told me she was leaving college. Later, when I asked one of her friends where she had gone, they told me, "Well, she had to go to Stockbridge." I was so unconscious I didn't realize that she was troubled; I found out later that Stockbridge was where you went if you were wealthy and had a "nervous breakdown."

I was assigned a second roommate. By now I realized that Vassar always put Jewish girls together. Later I learned about the quotas that had made it easier for me to get admitted, coming from Minnesota, than it was for Jewish girls from the eastern seaboard—especially New York. While I was at Vassar, fewer than eight percent of the students were Jewish. There was no Jewish club of any kind on the campus. I learned later that one of the freshman Jewish girls who had been assigned to room with a non-Jewish girl had been made to move. The Gentile girl's mother objected to her daughter having a Jewish roommate, the warden explained to the Jewish student. And, yes, it was the Jewish girl who had to accept the less desirable room.

My new roommate, Marge, had gone to Fieldston, a very competitive prep school in Manhattan. She considered me a real hayseed—a country bumpkin—and hardly deigned to speak to me. She wanted to stay up until midnight to study, while I liked the lights to be out by ten. I got up early and she slept late. My dream of having a roommate who might take me to visit New York City died quickly. Of course, freshmen weren't allowed to leave the campus until after Christmas, anyway.

My Midwestern drawl, especially the nasal way I pronounced the letter "a" in words like *bath*, annoyed somebody, I'm not sure who, so I was required to sign up for a noncredit course called Oral English. My fellow students included two from the deep South and three or four foreign students. We met in a little attic room in one of the older buildings on campus, where our instructor, Miss Ramsey, tried her best to make us speak standard American English, which she equated with the diction of Franklin D. Roosevelt. She had some primitive equipment for recording our voices; listening to myself for the first time was indeed a horrible experience. She had us reciting tongue twisters such as, "The witch had a wen on her hand; which witch?" I was also told to say "new" as if it were spelled "nyu" not "noo." I somehow completed this course, which I had never signed up for, without sounding much different to myself. Later, during my junior year, I wrote and broadcast radio scripts on the Vassar radio program, so apparently my diction was acceptable even among the patricians of the East Coast.

In late fall of my freshman year, I went to the warden, who was in charge of all social arrangements at the college, and begged for a single room. My wish would be granted after Christmas. I took my one trip home that year during the two-week Christmas break. I knew it wouldn't make sense financially or otherwise to spend most of four days on a train during the spring break, which would be only one week long. My provisional grades the fall semester had been a "B" average so I went back to my single room in North Tower considerably reassured about my college career.

My attitude toward Judaism at that time remained as it was after confirmation. I simply wasn't interested in anything Jewish or in learning about Judaism. I wanted to be a citizen of the world.

By spring I had found a good friend in my class, Betty Schnee, who did take me to visit her family in Manhattan. Betty had a sweet face with brown eyes, soft cheeks, and full lips. She was grossly overweight because of glandular problems, but her mind was acute. She smoked a lot, and took it on herself to get me through French—drilling me and helping me understand the grammar while she puffed away, waiting for me to give the right answers. Her ambition was to go to medical school, which she finally did. I made other friends and felt comfortable on the campus. We formed a poetry society. I later published in *The Little Magazine*, a campus publication.

The winter was mild, and I enjoyed looking out my eighth-floor window at the Catskills. I was told that Edna St. Vincent Millay had lived in my tower and written the famous lines:

> *All I could see from where I stood*
> *was three tall mountains and a wood...*

while taking in this view. I later learned that she had written the lines in her native Maine, but at the time, it meant a lot to me. I, too, was writing poetry in that tower. My heart was set on becoming a famous poet or possibly a novelist, and part of the reason I had chosen Vassar was that people like Millay had been educated there. It was a disappointment to me that Vassar had no writing courses in poetry, fiction or journalism. We were taught the history and criticism of literature and how to produce well-documented scholarly papers, but nothing beyond that.

I went home for summer vacation in a happy mood. By the spring of freshman year I knew I loved Vassar, the blossoming campus and the huge old trees, the talk that was about ideas (not boys), the invitations to a faculty person's house or having my professor to dinner at my dormitory, meeting girls from all over—foreign students, girls from California who rode western saddles and girls from New York who talked about "riding English" and dressage, girls who had lived in Europe and Asia, daughters of missionaries or State Department people, girls from New York City on scholarship living with others in co-op houses where they did the housework to save money. I admired the last as the brightest of our class and valued invitations to supper at their houses. It was a new wider world, exciting and welcoming, and I was growing into it.

Howard Brin, the tall redhead I had met in the train station in Chicago, had looked up my brother George soon after he arrived at Harvard for his freshman year; George was already a sophomore and was happy to tell Howard about his new school. Since Howard had a Harvard friend visiting the summer before our sophomore year, he invited George to come to a party and bring a certain girl. The problem was that the girl and my brother had quarreled the night before. Enter my mother, the woman of propriety. "You can't invite any girl at the last minute," she informed him. "You'll just have to take your sister." George was reluctant, but overruled.

I put on a new white dress with red trim and red shoes, went with my sulky brother, and met Howard Brin again. From that evening on, we began to go together.

By my junior year, Howard and I were becoming very close. He was a Zionist. My parents had had little interest in the settlement of what seemed to them to be a small desert country, quite hopeless and difficult to develop. They thought Jews were getting along very well in the United States. After Hitler became chancellor in Germany, they realized that Palestine was one important place of refuge—or would be if the British let the Jews come—and their attitude began to change. Howard's family, especially his grandfather, imbued him with the ideals of Zionism and of building a new national home for the Jewish people where they could develop free of oppression. His enthusiasm was contagious, but I remained full of questions. In addition, Howard's uncle had bought him a copy of Mordecai Kaplan's new book, *Judaism as a Civilization*, which dealt with the reconstruction and revitalization of Judaism and the Jewish people in America, Palestine, and the rest of the world. One weekend Howard met me in Manhattan and took me to hear Dr. Kaplan preach at the Society for the Advancement of Judaism. I was impressed, but not converted.

Besides English, economics, and politics, I found I had a free elective during my junior year and was wondering what to take. An older friend told me that one of the best courses she had ever taken at Vassar was called "The Bible as Literature," taught by Dr. Florence Lovell. I signed up for this course, which turned out to be a seminar with only seven students. Mrs. Lovell—a small, gray-haired woman, not at all imposing—was an inspiring teacher. She had a genuine love of the Bible, of the Jewish people, and of Hebrew literature. One of the great trips of her life had been a summer she had spent in Palestine. To have a Christian scholar truly admire Judaism was a new experience for me. Between her and Howard, who showed up regularly at Vassar College for weekends and invited me to the Harvard-Yale game and other events, my attitudes toward being Jewish began to change. I started what became a lifelong study of Jewish texts, history and culture.

While Vassar led me back toward Judaism, it didn't do as much for my writing career as I had dreamed when I chose it. I learned that Edna St. Vincent Millay had never graduated but had been expelled for staying out all night. My Vassar radio experience helped me get a summer job with a radio station, WMIN, in St. Paul. Everything was written out in those days; there was no ad libbing as there is now. I wrote commercials and announcements and had my own program for young women, then known as girls, called "Size 11." Even junior sizes were different then; nine was about the smallest and eleven was for a very slender girl. The program featured copy similar to stories in the new magazine *Mademoiselle,* popular music, and commercials from women's clothing stores like Field Schlick. I also wrote some dramas for Bee Baxter, a well-known radio personality in St. Paul at that time.

But my true love was poetry. I didn't major in English. I never felt I could catch up to the background in English literature of the girls from the prep schools. Besides, when I entered the class in Old English, a required course, it sounded like gibberish, and the instructor looked as though she had been born before Beowulf. I dropped out and majored in political science, which required fewer courses than English. I could take philosophy, economics, religion, government courses, and plenty of literature, too; there was Beowulf to Johnson, Blake to Keats, modern poets, and so forth. My favorite reading was

Untermeyer's anthology of modern poetry.

Junior year, besides the academic papers required, I submitted poetry to my English professor, Miss Swain. I wrote parodies or imitations of many of the romantic and later poets that we studied. It was good practice, and her comments were minimal. She was much more interested in having me write about the lives and historical periods of the writers we were studying, and about trends like the shift from classicism to romanticism, as illustrated by various writers.

But Vassar wasn't all academics. There were plays put on by the leftist drama department under Hallie Flanagan. There were dances and Outing Club expeditions to places like the Adirondacks. I made many friends, and continue to correspond with and visit Ruth Felmus, Sally Luther, and Charlotte Muller. Until their early deaths, I also kept up my friendships with Betty Schnee and Patricia Alden Smith.

Inviting Howard and sometimes my brother George to a weekend at Vassar created a happy situation. I learned about East Coast dance customs: formal clothes. The girls in long dresses and white gloves, the men in tails. We filled out dance cards, arranging with whom we and our dates would dance, before the men arrived. Couples entered the ballroom at Students' Building in a grand march led by posts (I learned that a post was a freshman who was not coming to the dance, but who nonetheless appeared in a long gown); the music was Big Band style. We danced the waltz and fox-trot, open steps and dips.

The next morning, Sunday, we took our dates on a walk by Wappinger's Creek or went to the Cider Mill for cider or, if someone had a car (not allowed for Vassar students), we might go for lunch and a beer. Men were not allowed in our rooms, nor did the landladies from whom we rented rooms for our dates allow us in their houses. The men had to leave in the afternoon. Of course it was romantic, but for me there was a major touch of realism—Howard had no car and had to find rides with someone else who was coming to Vassar. Frequently he ended up in a rumble seat, and almost always my heroic date arrived white and shaking with car sickness, a martyr to romance and to his fellow students' wild driving over the mountains to Poughkeepsie.

I left Vassar with friends, an ability to research almost anything except maybe physics or math, a decent background in English literature, some understanding of economics and government, as well as a reawakened interest in Judaism.

I also left Vassar in 1941 at the age of twenty with a Phi Beta Kappa key, an engagement ring on my left hand, and what had been diagnosed as an ulcer, but wasn't. Howard and I were convinced that war was around the corner; our parents were convinced that the draft would last for only a year and that we should postpone marriage. My parents drove east for the graduation; afterwards they took me and Howard to Montreal to buy blankets and china for my trousseau. We arrived in good spirits in what seemed like a foreign country; Dad outwitted a trooper who stopped him for speeding by pretending not to understand French. Howard's graduation was two weeks later than mine, so he took a train to Boston from Albany, meeting his own family in Cambridge, while we drove home. I am not sure how we did it, but Howard and I prevailed over our four strong-minded parents and were married on August 6, 1941. I was twenty and Howard was twenty-one.

Howard had a fairly high draft number, so we settled into

an apartment at 3220 Girard Avenue South in Minneapolis after a joyful honeymoon trip. Howard started working at a lowly position at the Brin Glass Company, which had been founded by his father early in the century. Howard got a ride to work every morning from his uncle because we couldn't afford a car. We had two Schwinn bikes that we bought with wedding gift money.

I had started to write a novel even though I had no idea how to do it. In 1941, my mother persuaded me to join her in a writing class taught by Meridel Le Sueur at the St. Paul YWCA. It was one of the most wonderful things Mother ever did for me.

Meridel Le Sueur was a striking woman, with piercing dark eyes and black hair. She often wore American Indian jewelry, and I remember her draped in Navajo weavings. She was a political radical, always supporting the working class, and telling us how the Middle West had been colonized by the capitalists of the East Coast, an idea she developed in her book, *North Star Country*. Howard, studying labor economics at Harvard, and I at Vassar with American Student Union connections, both considered ourselves radical. Even before hearing her on writing, I admired Meridel.

She had developed her own excellent methods to teach writing, methods which were imitated or discovered decades later by other teachers. First, she taught us to write notes, saying, "Be free, write anything you can think of, your feelings, your ideas, your experiences, let it flow. Don't worry about grammar and spelling." This is now usually called journaling. She also taught us to observe and note details of clothing, rooms, scenes, and to sit in streetcars listening to the speech of ordinary people and writing it down when we could. After that, we needed to learn how to go over a mass of these notes to select scenes, themes, conversations that could be the germs of a story. A story had to have drama, conflict, a beginning, a dénouement, and an end. It did NOT need documentation, footnotes, bibliography or even development along logical paths. I was freed of the constraints of the academic paper and ready to move into writing fiction, poetry, or journalism with some excitement to it.

Meanwhile, I had purchased a cookbook and was trying to learn to cook. The first day in my apartment I had phoned Mother and asked her how to make a pot roast with carrots and potatoes. Her theory had always been that anyone could learn to cook if she knew how to read; I thought basting was something you did to a hem and not to a roast. I found a part-time job doing some public relations for the Minneapolis Girl Scout office, radio presentations for the senior girls to do, and posters and news articles. I worked on my novel. Every Friday night we put on our formal clothes and went to dinner and the symphony with the Brins, and every Sunday evening we put on our informal clothes and had supper in St. Paul with the Firestones. On a few weekends in the summer, we managed to go to Bone Lake with them. Besides working, Howard took a class in toolmaking at Miller Vocational High School so that when he was drafted he could be assigned to army ordnance. He had always liked both mechanics and woodworking so he hoped this course would qualify him.

My brother George was living at home, going to medical school. He had been born December 6, 1918, while Howard's birthday was December 6, 1919. On Sunday, December 7, 1941, we got the families together to celebrate the birthdays, but instead we found ourselves glued to the radio, listening to accounts of Pearl Harbor.

The war had begun.

18

The War and After

All our friends began to leave for the war. There were new government and defense jobs, the Army, Navy, Air Force and Marine Corps were taking draftees and enlistees as fast as possible. Howard discovered that if he waited to be drafted, he could not choose his branch of the service. After a few months, Howard enlisted in Army ordnance and was sent to Aberdeen Proving Ground in Aberdeen, Maryland, for thirteen weeks of basic training. When he finished and could get an occasional pass to leave the post, I moved to Washington, D.C., the closest place I could find a job.

I worked for the War Production Board (WPB), the agency that was shifting important materials from civilian to armed services uses. Automobile companies were now producing tanks and jeeps, so they needed steel and rubber. The textile industry began producing sheets, blankets, and uniforms for the army and navy; the leather industry, shoes and belts; the natural gas industry, energy to run war factories; the chemical, food, and just about every industry joined in. WPB set up divisions for every major commodity, staffed by people from industry and the military. We received applications for material and made allocations to the various services as well as to civilian needs. Many food items, like meat and butter, and consumer goods, like shoes, gasoline, and sugar, were rationed.

I was employed in personnel, interviewing people from file clerks to generals, and writing descriptions of their jobs. When a new item needed to be allocated, I set up an entire dummy division; then placement hired people to perform the jobs I had described. Six months later, I interviewed the new employees to see how the organization actually worked. If a supervisor wanted to give someone a raise, whether a chemist or a messenger, I had to interview the person, write a job description, and argue with the Civil Service Commission about the classification of the job. I was a cog in the machine that was running the U.S. economy and my work was fascinating, even if I did have to learn to write bureaucratese.

There were no apartments to be rented, so I rented a bedroom in the brick house of a Mrs. Smith on Rhode Island Avenue. I was allowed to fix breakfast in her kitchen but no other meal. Some evenings after work when I'd had a note from Howard, I went directly to the Union Depot, a cathedral to transport, like so many railroad stations were in those days. Light shone through the ceiling high above the scurrying people; trains arrived and departed from all directions. I'd sit on a bench and look for a tall redhead in the khakis of an enlisted man. The station seemed to have hundreds of soldiers hurrying past. In their regulation caps and short haircuts, I couldn't tell them apart. Sailors in whites would rush by, I'd half get up, thinking I saw my husband, then sit down again. And then Howard would appear, it seemed, out of nowhere. We'd hug and rush off to a restaurant for supper—we liked one near the depot called the Chinese Lantern. We'd talk and laugh and try to tell each other everything at once.

Afterwards, we'd go "home" to my room, where Mrs. Smith once mumbled her doubts that we were really married. We closed the door, enjoyed ourselves, and went off to sleep early, after setting the alarm so that Howard could get up again at 2 a.m. to return for reveille in his barracks on the post at 5 a.m.

I still have a big notebook full of notes à la Meridel that I managed to keep between seeing Howard and working a six-day week. I kept writing after he finished officer's training and went overseas to England.

Howard would be in the army "for the duration," which seemed as if it might last forever. When would we invade Fortress Europe? Could the Russians hold out? We were able to supply them only through the far northern port of Murmansk; to get there our ships had to run through the submarine-infested North Sea. Like every army wife I hoped for V-mail every day, but I didn't always get it. I wrote as often as I could, almost daily, followed the war news with clenched fists, and cried into my pillow at night. Would Howard ever come home to me? Working long hours, thinking I was helping the war effort, dreaming of having a husband and family in the "wonderful postwar world" kept me going.

By some strange series of events, Howard was transferred to Long Beach Ordnance Depot in California. I quit my job to join him; by then, the war in Europe was winding down, but the Japanese were putting up a tremendous fight. I was pregnant on that wonderful day in August 1945 when we went to

Hollywood and Vine to see everyone cheering and laughing, a happy mob because at last it was V-J (Victory in Japan) Day. The war was over, but it would be 1946 before Howard was officially released from the service. A personal thrill in August, 1945, was the first publication of one of my short stories in what I thought of as a real magazine. I had been keeping card files of stories and poems submitted widely for quite a while. Now there was some sense to my accumulation of rejection slips.

Our long awaited first child, Judith Rosalie, was born in November 1945 in Los Angeles. I had begun my postwar life of family and writing. When Judy was eight weeks old, inhabiting a little basket, we took the train (all three of us in a lower berth) to Minneapolis. We had hoped for a vacation but found that Howard's father was seriously ill. Howard would soon have to manage the company that not only supported his mother, his three uncles (who worked there), and their families, but also assisted his brother and sister.

No civilian housing had been built during the war; we discovered that there were no rentals to be had as soon as we arrived home, so we stayed with Howard's parents, then shifted to my parents' home, and began trying to buy a house. Demand was high and houses were few. Howard came rushing in one afternoon and said we could look at a bungalow on Aldrich Avenue South near 36th Street. I wrapped up the baby and we drove in his father's car to what looked like a simple story and a half house built perhaps forty or fifty years before in a middle- or working-class neighborhood. It was being shown by a young Norwegian real estate agent. The couple who were selling the house were of French-Canadian origin; he was a truck driver and she was a housewife with two children. When she heard our last name, she asked if we were Jewish. We said we were.

"I've heard your mother speak," she told Howard. "I know she's a fine woman, but we can't sell this house to you. After all, it's in St. Leonard's parish."

Howard smiled, "All of Minneapolis—in fact all of Minnesota—is divided into parishes by the Catholic church," Howard said. "Besides, this home is just six blocks from our synagogue on 34th and Dupont."

"I'm sorry," she said, "but we're friends with people in the neighborhood, and they'd never forgive us if we sold to Jews."

"But you're moving away," I said. I saw that her burly dark-haired husband was nodding in agreement with her.

She turned to me. "They wouldn't let their children play with your child," she said. "I couldn't do that to you."

Howard spoke up. "That's some time away," he told her, "and we can deal with it."

Again she refused. The real estate agent was angry. "This man," he said, "is wearing the uniform of his country (he pointed at Howard who wore the silver bars of a first lieutenant and his overseas ribbons) and has fought for our freedom. How can you refuse him?"

"They wouldn't be happy here," the woman replied. The agent told her he wouldn't bring anyone else to see her house, and then we left. Howard sighed, what I still think of as a deep Jewish sigh, and said, "Nothing has changed."

A couple of days later he rushed in, telling me an agent would hold a house in St. Louis Park until we got there. While a line of eager buyers formed outside, we bought a four room house, white with blue shutters, at 2937 Edgewood. It had a big kitchen, living room, two little bedrooms, bathroom, full basement and garage. It would be our home for three years.

Our lives changed rapidly. Howard's father died in 1947 and soon his mother developed Parkinson's disease and required help. My brother Linn, with his wife Jean and son Roger, had come home from work in Washington to join my father's law practice in St. Paul. They added new partners. My brother George, home from the army with his wife Betty and son Bill, completed a residency at the Veterans Administration Hospital and moved to California.

I kept on writing, often at night, and occasionally published a story or poem. Our son Aaron Daniel, at first called Arthur Daniel, was born in September 1948. In 1949 we built a four-bedroom house at 2861 Burnham Boulevard, overlooking Cedar Lake, the family home until 1992. Howard loved building and took an active role in the planning and construction of the house, adding the extra storage I was sure I would need. Our son David Milton was born in September 1950. But our happiness could not be complete because my father became seriously ill soon after the baby's birth.

I remember driving home from the hospital in very slow traffic on Franklin Avenue, unable to see much because of the huge wet snowflakes hitting the windshield and my tears smearing my glasses. My father died when David was a cheerful toddler, twenty months old. Now once more I tried to be the friend or the sister my mother had always wanted, but it wasn't easy with three little ones. The freeway hadn't been built; it was still a 45-minute drive from one home to the other. We were a one-car family; I could drive Howard to work, get a baby-sitter, and have the car for the day, then pick him up with three fussy kids in the backseat. Luckily, Mother drove and continued many of her volunteer activities, although we knew she had angina.

We had always wanted four children and I became pregnant again, expecting my baby at the end of December 1953. At the beginning of October I was sitting on the couch reading when I realized my bag of waters had broken. I called the doctor immediately.

"You'll probably go into labor within twenty-four hours," he said, "and babies delivered this early are seldom viable."

"Oh," I answered weakly, "You mean I'm having a miscarriage."

"I'm afraid so. But stay in bed; if labor is delayed a few days, it would help. Call me if there's any change. Sometimes there's a miracle."

My first thought was for my other children. Judy was eight, a third-grader with big brown eyes who loved dance more than anything. She was hoping for a baby sister. Aaron, my sturdy kindergartner, now called Arthy, was taking life seriously but not David, (now Deedee) my bubbly three year old, who liked his morning nursery school. How would I explain to them that I had to stay in bed and that there might not be a baby? I got on the phone to Howard first and then to find someone to come in to care for the older children while I lay in bed. And I didn't go into labor for several days.

The first miracle happened. My little girl, weighing two pounds and five ounces, a little over eleven weeks before her due date, was born alive. Everything was quiet in the delivery room. The obstetrician and the pediatrician Dr. Herschel Kaufman, stood bending over a table, working on the silent baby. No squawk or cry like those I'd heard when the others were born.

"She's breathing!" Herschel exclaimed. He gathered what looked like a bundle of blankets and rushed out. "Going to the preemie nursery," a nurse told me as she finally took me down from the stirrups. I hadn't seen my baby, nor touched her. In the course of raising my first three, Herschel had become a dear friend, loving the children and loved by them in turn. Now he held the key to my hopes and fears for this new child.

The next morning I was taken to see my baby—that is, I was left in the hall to look through the glass door of an office into the glass door of the nursery at a tiny baby in a glass box with electric wires and oxygen tubes going into it. This device was an Isolette, with controlled heat, humidity, and oxygen. The nurses put their hands through "portholes" covered with plastic to care for the infants.

She lay on her back, head lower than her body to keep phlegm from going down her throat, a nurse explained. She was red and wrinkled, kicking her unbelievably tiny feet very fast. She had a little bit of black hair but no finger- or toenails. Her tiny head, wrinkled and red, fitted between the nurse's thumb and forefinger. I couldn't see all of her face beneath the adhesive that held a nasal feeding tube in place. She had a human baby face, except that her nose was so flat that I could see only the little nostrils. She threw her tiny arm up over her head. It was no thicker than one of my fingers and so devoid of any flesh that it looked like an anatomy student's drawing. I could see two tiny strips of muscle vibrating under that thin red skin. She looked like a miniature caricature of a starvation victim, and I found it hard to believe she could live. She was less than fifteen inches long and expected to lose weight for a few days.

"What weight?" I wondered.

She did lose, stabilizing at a little under two pounds, while I was still in the hospital for the routine five-day stay. Herschel explained that he had read an article recently indicating that the cause of blindness, so common in premature babies, might be too much oxygen, so he was reducing it but being careful not to reduce it too much. Too little, I discovered, might produce brain damage. I was also told that many premature babies had heart defects. I saw her looking more skeletal every day and wondered what my life would be like with a defective child, or if she would survive long enough for us to love her, and then…

Soon I was home with no baby to nurse at night or in the early hours. I could sleep all night and, as I recovered and began to get good reports from the hospital, I became a demon housekeeper and cleaned everything in sight. This was anything but my usual behavior! My kindergartner was protective. The first time I dropped him off at school on my way to visit the baby, he asked, "Did the doctor *say* you could drive, Mommy?" and "This baby business is hard for you… maybe we have enough babies in this family."

We named the baby Deborah Johanna; she was taken off the feeding tube, and while she didn't really suck, the nurses could feed her by filling her mouth with formula from a nipple with big holes in it. She'd swallow. She began to regulate her own temperature and was taken out of the Isolette. Now she was breathing ordinary air and not turning blue. When she got to be four pounds, the doctor began to talk about sending her home.

I took the children to the dentist, the barber, and the shoe store. I painted a new chest of drawers for David and scrubbed his old one for the baby. I painted the crib, which had needed it ever since Judy chewed on a railing. There was a small room we had used for a playroom right behind the kitchen. Above the sink was a pass-through with a wooden sliding door, which we replaced with a sliding glass door. I could use that room for a nursery and still see the baby when I was in the kitchen. I polished off my PTA calling list, drove all my carpools, went on a diet, and got a haircut. I went to the hospital, scrubbed up, and held my fragile little one for the first time, feeding her and learning about her special care from the nurses.

When Debbie came home she weighed four-and-a-half pounds and wasn't even due to be born for another five weeks. I fed her—she still didn't suck, but she did swallow—two ounces every three hours around the clock. When we left Northwestern Hospital, Mrs. Gandell, the head nurse of the preemie nursery, told me Debbie was the smallest normal baby ever to leave the hospital. The nurse wanted to be invited to Debbie's wedding! (When, instead, I invited Mrs. Gandell to Deborah's bat mitzvah thirteen years later, she said Debbie was *still* the smallest normal baby ever to leave Northwestern's preemie nursery.)

But what was normal? This baby didn't act startled or cry when she heard a loud noise; she didn't even blink if I flashed a light in her eyes. She almost never cried; it was hard to tell if she was awake or asleep. Her eyes might roll up in her head or open or close, but they didn't focus.

At first the other children watched her through the glass door. After about a week, I allowed them in the nursery. Judy said, "My sweet baby sister." Arthy agreed, "Yes, she's a sweet baby sister." Dedee announced, "She smells like cooked cereal."

Our first year with Debbie was one of crises. She turned blue—I saw her from the kitchen and worked on her to start her breathing again while Howard called the fire department. The cause? Maybe no reflex to cough up phlegm. If it had happened at night—a crib death. We didn't know for many weeks whether she could hear or see, but finally, some time after her due date, when she weighed about eight pounds, she began to behave like a newborn, crying when the kids were noisy and blinking at lights, sucking away on a regular bottle and waking at night for feedings. She caught chicken pox and began projectile vomiting. For a few weeks I cleaned vomit off the baby and me, the ceiling and floor, and fed her again. Usually the second time, it stayed down. Of course her development was slow, but when she learned to crawl at about a year, she found a screw under her father's workbench to swallow, and got up on the kitchen counter to sample the aspirin. But at last, by the time she was three and a half or four, she was like other little girls her age.

Deborah was a miracle, but in watching her develop, I understood that all of my children—their lives, their talents, their health—were miracles. Children are a gift; for that gift, I was and am grateful to God. Debbie's birth greatly intensified my search for the divine. Poetry is about death and birth, decay and creation, about love and faith. Even before the blessing of Debbie's life, I lived amidst these experiences, driven to write, although I often had to get up in the middle of the night to do it.

At that time I found the rabbi of our synagogue, Stanley Rabinowitz, to be an inspiration. He learned that I read poetry and asked me to find material he could include in services on Friday nights at the Adath Jeshurun Synagogue. In the 1950s very little liturgical poetry was being written by Christians or Jews; after failing to find anything appropriate, I began to write responsive and unison readings for him. He became a mentor for me, and suggested a project of writing an interpretation for each portion of the Torah (the five books of Moses). He directed my reading, taught me a great deal about Judaism, and encouraged my writing. During his seven years in Minneapolis, I concentrated on personal poetry and liturgy.

My first book of poems, *A Time to Search*, was published by Jonathan David, New York, in 1959. I was delighted by this accomplishment, but at the same time, it was a sad day when the box of books arrived one morning while I was home alone. I wanted to call my mother to tell her, but I couldn't, because a heart attack had killed her two years before.

After Rabbi Rabinowitz left Minneapolis, I worked less intensively with Rabbis Jerome Lipnick, Arnold Goodman, and Bernard Raskas. I published poetry and articles extensively in *The Reconstructionist Magazine* and other periodicals. I was, as far as I know, the first woman to have her work included in the prayerbooks of the major liberal movements—Conservative, Reform and Reconstructionist.

When we first settled in Minneapolis after the war, I found bittersweet in hedges and ditches along county roads west of the city; every fall I went to pick some as I had in my childhood. Bittersweet meant harvest and thanksgiving, sunshine, even in the winter; it meant my mother's steadfast belief that the world could be a better and more beautiful place and that we could help make it so, an idea known in Judaism as "tikkun olam." After a while, my secret places were purchased by developers and houses were built where there had been farms and woods.

Bone Lake, too, began to look suburban, with houses crowded all along the lakeshore, even on swampy land where my father had claimed nobody with any sense would build. After his death, the place was sold, no longer wilderness, just one cabin among many, whose new owners installed electricity and plumbing. Now I have to buy bittersweet at a flower shop, and it never seems as bright.

As our children grew, my husband built a sukkah, something neither of us had had in our childhood homes, to celebrate the autumn festival of Sukkot, that follows the High Holy Days. It is a thanksgiving and harvest festival, and normally a little booth is built outdoors and decorated with fruits and vegetables hung from its roof, open to the sky. Shocks of corn or other grain and children's drawings decorate the walls. In cold Minnesota, our sukkah was a bower over our dining room table, and it was always decorated with bittersweet. My parents hadn't needed a sukkah to teach us to give thanks for nature's bounty in the fall, to make the transition to school and work, and to learn a love of nature. The human heart finds its ways, celebrating and adapting old traditions, or making new ones.

As we grew older, we traveled a great deal, especially to Israel, where all six of us went, in 1963. We stopped in Europe as well. It is good to belong to an ancient and worldwide community, to be at home in synagogues in places as remote from each other as Morocco, Costa Rica, Prague, Curaçao, and Israel. It is even better to work toward a set of ethical imperatives based on justice in this world, as first proclaimed by the prophets.

Being Jewish presented Howard and me with the opportunity, method, and incentive to build a loving family and to work toward a caring community. Within our long, varied tradition we found many ways to celebrate, worship, and search for God in the universe, in humanity, and in ourselves. Most of all, being Jewish set me on a path that led me to moments when I truly felt the presence of God. This is what I wrote when I first felt that presence:

GOD OF MEN AND MOUNTAINS

God of men and mountains,
Master of people and planets,
Creator of the universe:
I am afraid.

I am afraid of the angels
Thou has sent to wrestle with me:

The angel of success
Who carries a two-edged sword,

The angels of darkness
Whose names I do not know,

The angel of death
For whom I have no answer.

I am afraid of the touch
Of Thy great hand on my feeble heart.

Yet must I turn to Thee and praise Thee
Awful and great though Thou art
For there is none else.

There is no strength nor courage
But in Thee.
There is no life, no light, no joy
But in Thee.